EVERLASTING FLOWERS

edited by
Moyna McWilliam
and Dorothy Shipman

Marshall Cavendish London & New York

Published by
Marshall Cavendish Publications Limited,
58, Old Compton Street,
London W1V 5PA

© Marshall Cavendish Limited 1973, 1974, 1975, 1976

First printing 1976

ISBN 0 85685 170 1

Printed in Great Britain by Redwood Burn Limited.

Some of this material has previously appeared in
other Marshall Cavendish publications.

Introduction

The short and expensive life of fresh flowers makes them a luxury for any home – not least of all in the winter months when you cannot simply pick them from the garden. However, by thinking ahead and preserving flowers during the summer, you can ensure that you have colourful and everlasting arrangements and decorations all the year round.

Starting with dried flowers, leaves and seed heads, advice is given on which varieties to grow, when to plant, and most important of all, when to pick them. Many different methods of drying and preserving are then given, with hints and tips from experts on the best way to treat each type of material. And you will be surprised by the many uses that dried flowers, with no need for water, can be put – not just in arrangements but in various forms to decorate corners through the house. From cones, domes and pyramids to more conventional pictures and plaques, lots of unusual ideas are given, including crystallizing flowers for decorating flowers and sweets.

How to preserve the scents of flowers are also dealt with – from delicious spicy pomanders to sweetly scented pot-pourri, sachets and pillows.

The final section is devoted to pressed flowercraft – how to press for the most successful results and how best to use your materials to decorate the house – from delicately hued flower pictures and plaques to the most practical items such as trays, place-mats and paperweights.

Flowers give a distinctive touch to any home – and what could be better for an original gift than flowers which, with a little care, would give year round decoration.

Contents

Picked by Albert at the Fort Aug: 18 à Octreoille. Cherbourg 1857

From   Cherbourg —

From Cherbourg — Aug: 18 - 1854

Flowers in the past

The transient and fragile nature of flowers makes it difficult to trace when and where they were first preserved but we do know that flowers have always played an important role in the lives of men. From the very earliest times, as ancient records show, they have been given as tokens of our love for the living and our respect for the dead, and have served in religious rituals of the greatest importance.

In the British Museum, London, is an example of some of the earliest remains of preserved flowers in the form of a garland taken from a Roman tomb in Hawara, Egypt, and estimated to be about 2000 years old. Although the colours of these flowers have long since faded, their beauty is still intact, captured in their creamy folds.

By the middle ages, sheaves of wheat were brought into the house for decorative and religious purposes and one can only speculate that this might have been the beginning of using preserved material as a form of decoration. At the same time, man began investigating the world in which he lived. As a result, beautiful books of pressed flower samples, taken from botanical studies, remain, their colours still bright although the flowers themselves have been dead for six hundred years.

The ninth edition of the Encyclopedia Britannica, published about 1891, tells us that everlasting flowers were cultivated on a large scale in the Mediterranean areas and were sold in Paris.

But it was in Victorian England that everlasting flowercraft enjoyed most popularity. It takes little imagination to picture the young ladies of the day, out for a leisurely walk with their governesses, being instructed in the recording and collecting of botanical specimens, and carefully pressing their finds.

Queen Victoria's own album 'Flowers-Souvenirs' was recently on sale. It is interesting to note that most of the flowers pressed by the Queen were associated with death, her souvenirs kept in loving memory of her husband. She pressed flowers from the ones that lay on his bed during his last illness and leaves taken from a wreath given by the princesses. She also brought back and preserved flowers from the Royal Mausoleum at Frogmore.

By the early twentieth century potted palms, ferns and pampas grass had moved into vogue in the fashionable town houses. However, it was still quite common to see dried grasses, gypsophila and helichrysums in the windows of cottages in the country.

After the second world war, we entered a sad period where everywhere one looked, one saw evidence of the mass production of plastic flowers, which had neither natural beauty nor served as a medium for artistic expression. Fortunately, this trend is now passing and we are returning to the use of natural plant material. The new awareness of preserving flowers, leaves and seed heads has never been more popular and appreciated, and there is an ever-increasing flow of new ideas with which to use this preserved material to advantage in the home.

Opposite Collecting and pressing flowers was a favourite pastime in Victorian England—the Queen herself keeping a book of flower souvenirs, mainly in remembrance of her husband, Albert. This page shows carefully pressed specimens collected by Albert from Cherbourg in 1857. However, not all Victorian uses for dried and pressed flowers were so morbid. Young ladies of the day would have pressed and retained flower mementoes given and received in love left and a favourite use for preserved materials was to decorate paintings, usually to depict a garden or country scene.

Everlasting flowers

When winter comes and the garden is looking sorry for itself, the search for materials to brighten up the home becomes, inevitably, more difficult; and the widespread use of central heating has made the life of bought fresh flowers short and rather expensive. However, if you have planned ahead by growing and drying some decorative summer flowers, you will be able to fill your home with attractive flower arrangements, not just during the winter months, but throughout the whole year.

Success in the use of dried flowers relies to a great extent in treating them totally separately from fresh flowers—each should be accepted on its own merits. Fresh flowers are always appreciated for what they are—beautiful examples of plant life that add a touch of luxury to any room. Preserved flowers have a charm of their own and by their everlasting nature can be put to many beautiful and varied uses.

Experimenting with varieties
The range of flowers for preserving is immense, ranging from true everlastings such as the popular Helichrysum bracteatum (the strawflower) to the softer varieties such as delphiniums, roses and sunflowers. The varieties given are the ones that take most easily to being dried, but there is always ample scope for experiment. Trial and error will bring some failures, of course, but also success and originality to your displays.

Colour changes
Sometimes during the process of preservation the flowers will lose a little of their natural bright colour, only to take on a more subtle shade that somehow still seems to contrast favourably with dull, winter days. This does not apply to all the flowers—Helipterum roseum and statice sinuatum will retain their brilliant colours, giving a wide choice of materials to work with.

Leaves preserved with glycerine, although retaining their flexibility, will also undergo a colour change ranging from a pale cream to a deep brown, depending upon the type of leaf being treated. If green or grey leaves are desired they can be pressed or dried in a dessicant such as silica gel or borax.

The material which is most easily adapted is of course dried grass. The bright primary colours available from florists can add life to an otherwise dull arrangement. However, there are means by which grasses can be dyed in the home with considerable success and although their colour is perhaps not so vivid as those available in shops, their subtlety is often far more effective.

Using dried materials
With the growing popularity of preserving flowers, many ideas have been devised to use their beauty in the home. Apart from arrangements, their flexibility enables them to be made into long-lasting collages and flower pictures, flower balls and pendants, festive decorations and to create unusual paper-weights.

In fact, they can be used, in many different forms, throughout the whole house, to enhance, brighten and add visual interest to every room.

For beauty alone, dried flowers can never rival fresh, but for the best results, each should be accepted on their own merits. Dried flowers have a charm and attractiveness of their own and their malleability means that they can be used not just in arrangements, but to decorate items for the house. Calendars, plaques and pictures are a few of the projects which can be made with dried flowers and, grasses, although very attractive in their natural colours, can be easily dyed to add colour to an arrangement.

Choosing flowers

You do not have to own a garden in order to collect flowers, so long as you can go out into the countryside to pick some. One word of warning though; many varieties of plants are becoming increasingly rare, so before picking, make sure that the flower is well-established and be sure not to uproot the plant.

If you are lucky enough to have a garden then your choice of flowers is infinitely wider. Many flowers are grown especially for drying, and add summer colour to the garden as well as forming attractive decorations for the winter.

There is also the advantage of being able to pick the flowers at exactly the right time for drying to ensure the best possible results.

Flowers for drying

Flowers which will dry easily fall into two categories, the 'everlastings', or 'immortelles', and those called 'soft' flowers, some of which can be dried successfully if the process is quick.

True everlasting or immortelles

True everlastings or immortelles are those flowers grown specifically to be dried. They are mainly annuals and tend to grow best if planted in a sunny place.

Acrolinium roseum or *Helipterum roseum* [rose sunray] is a straw daisy with petals softer than those of its near relative *Helichrysum bracteatum*. It grows to about 61cm (2ft) tall and has daisy-like pink flowers of papery texture. There is also a white variety called *Helipterum album*. In a good summer it should flower six weeks after it has been sown, so you can grow and dry it in the same year.

Ammobium alatum grandiflorum (everlasting sand flower) [big wing everlasting] has silvery-white petals and a domed yellow centre. It does grow to 61cm (2ft) tall but its stems are short in proportion

to its flower heads and you may need to lengthen them when you come to arrange them.

The silvery grey foliaged *Anaphalis* (pearl everlasting) has clusters of tiny everlasting-type daisy flowers and grows to 30·5 to 60cm (1 to 2ft).

Gomphrena globosa (otherwise known as globe amaranth) was a favorite in Elizabethan gardens. It grows 30·5 to 46cm (12 to 18in) high, has white, pink or purple globular flowers and is half hardy.

Perhaps the best known of all the everlastings is *Helichrysum bracteatum* (the straw flower) which includes both 91·5 to 122cm (3 to 4ft tall) and shorter dwarf varieties. It has flowers rather like those of a stiff, shiny-petalled double daisy in an assortment of colours—orange, wine-red, apricot, yellow, gold and white. The flowers should be picked as soon as they begin to open.

Helipterum manglesii, also known as *Rhodanthe maglesii* [Margles sunray], grows from 30·5 to 46cm (12 to 18in) tall and has tiny daisy flowers in clusters of florets—white, pink or rose; both double and single blooms.

Statice (*Limonium*) *sinuatum* (sea lavender) [notchleaf] grows to 61cm (2ft) and has papery flowers in blue, mauve or white. Its perennial cousins are *Statice* (*Limonium*) *latifolium* which has mauve flowers —this is somewhat taller, reaching 61 to 92·5cm (2 to 3ft) and *Limonium bonduellii* [Algerian sea lavender] which has yellow flowers and grows from 30·5 to 61cm (1 to 2ft). Both of these dry equally well.

Xeranthemum is another everlasting with silvery pink, mauve or white flowers. It grows to 61cm (2ft) tall and must be sown where it is to flower as it resents being moved.

Above *A brightly coloured mass of
some of the more popular and easily
available everlastings.*
Left *Achillea, a yarrow, is one of the
most successful flowers for drying which
is not a true everlasting. The variety
shown is Achillea filipendulina, well
known for retaining its colour when
dried.*

Cultivation and harvesting

All these flowers revel in a hot dry summer and last longer in the house after a good season. If you have a greenhouse sow them in the early spring to get an early start, planting them six to eight weeks later. If not, sow in the sunniest spot in the garden in late spring, thinning the seedlings to 15cm (6in) apart, and hope for a dry summer.

Always be prepared to sacrifice garden decoration for winter display because these flowers for drying need to be cut just as they come to maturity. If they are left two or three days too long the petals are less closely folded over one another and they soon shatter once they are completely dry. Remember to cut them with as long stems as possible.

Other flowers you can dry

There are many other flowers easily bought as plants or grown from seed which—although not true everlastings—have flowers which can be dried successfully and which associate happily in arrangements with true 'immortelles'. With a little luck and a reasonable amount of care the most unexpected flowers can be dried—from golden rod and cornflowers to delphiniums, edelweiss, roses and sunflowers provided they are cut at the point of maturity and are not left too long. Here are some of the more suitable types.

Acanthus mollis (bear's breeches) with its tall spikes of white and purple flowers and large, jagged leaves grows to 122cm

Below *Helipterum manglesii*, also known as Rhodanthe manglesii, is an Australian everlasting that can be cultivated with care in most of the warmer climates. It has tiny daisy flowers in clusters of white, pink or rose coloured florets.
Bottom *Acrolinium roseum syn Helipterum roseum*—a well known straw daisy with softer petals than most everlastings. It can be grown and dried in the same year.
Right *Varieties of statice can be found growing wild along coasts and around salt marshes throughout the world.*

(4ft) and should be gathered when its lower florets are at their best. If you wait until these begin to fade the whole flower will fade and lose its colour.

Achillea is a yarrow which is found in many varieties from a few centimetres up to 152·5cm (5ft) tall. It has flat white or yellow heads made up of a mass of tiny flowers and feathery grey-green leaves. This dries very well, and keeps its colour.

Catananche (blue cupidone or cupid's dart) has large blue daisy-like flowers and grows 61 to 91·5cm (2 to 3ft) tall. It is one of the few which should be gathered and dried when it is fully developed.

The prickly thistle family includes the superb silver-green and blue *Eryngium maritimum* (Sea Holly) and the steely, blue metallic balls of *Echinops* (globe thistle). The thistle family as a whole provides a lot of interesting material in various sizes, all of which dry well and provide bold contrast to the more fragile daisies.

Hydrangeaceae (hydrangea) is dried most successfully if it is arranged in fresh water and then just forgotten and left. Pick it when it is just changing colour, from blue to green and pink to red. For some inexplicable reason one or two blooms usually fail to dry well—remove these immediately and keep the rest for arrangements.

Below *Catananche caerulea* is an excellent flower for drying. In the past it was often used in love potions, hence its common name, Cupid's dart or blue cupidone.
Left *Helichrysum bracteatum*, one of a large genus of plants ranging from alpines to shrubs. Helichrysum bracteatum is a native of Australia but can be cultivated in most areas with care. Other varieties are Helichrysum lanatum, with felted leaves and stems and yellow flowers, and Helichrysum vestitum, both natives of South Africa.

Right *Amaranthus Caudatus* (Love-lies-Bleeding) *a non-everlasting, which, along with* Amaranthus Hypochondriacus (Prince's feather), *can be dried successfully.*

Below right *The silvery-white and chaffy flowers of* Anaphalis nubigena. *The flowers of this plant can be dyed by the same method as for dried grasses to add extra colour to an arrangement.*

Below far right *Hydrangeas are dried most successfully if picked when just changing colour, arranged in fresh water and left to dry.*

Bottom *Echinops, a member of the thistle family, provide a bold contrast to the more fragile daisies.*

Bottom right *The flowers of* Eryngium oliverianum *surrounded by blue floral bracts.*

Seed heads

Many of our garden plants give us double value for they produce decorative seed heads and fruit as well as flowers or foliage. Some like physalis are grown for these alone.

Physalis franchettii [*physalis alkekengi*] (Chinese lantern, Cape Gooseberry). [Ground Cherry] grows to 61cm (2ft) and has orange lanterns covering its berries. Gather these when the first lanterns turn orange but before the first frosts or damp have got to them, the other pods will turn orange as they dry. Remove all the leaves before drying.

Dipsacus silvestris (Teasels) [Venus Cup]

are biennials. Pick in the late summer by streams and rivers or grow them from seed. *Dipsacus fullonium* (Fuller's Teasel) is a good tall one—122cm to 183cm (4 to 6ft)—and they all dry superbly.

Another biennial is *Lunaria* (Honesty) varieties of which grow to between 46cm and 91·5cm (1½ to 3ft). This is a really good plant as it has white or purple flowers in spring, and through the summer its flat oval seed-pods go from a plummy-green to silvery-white thus being useful for flower arrangements all through the year. Gather it when the pods begin to change colour

Below *The thistle family provides many varied and interesting seed heads for arrangements. Dipsacus sylvestris, the common teasel, is probably the most popular, growing to a height of 1·8m (6 ft).*
Below left *The papery seed heads of Lunaria annua. These should be picked when they are just changing colour to prevent the delicate seed pods being damaged.*

—if you leave the pods to turn white on the plant, they will probably become brittle and damaged. Alternatively, young green pods can be dried and used entire to give colour to an arrangement. These also glycerine well if preserved early in the season.

Moluccella laevis (Bells of Ireland) [Asian molucca balm] is a good and quite distinctive half-hardy annual. It grows to 91·5cm (3ft), and has tiny, shell-like flowers with bell-like sheaths, growing in whorls and spirals around the stems, which turn cream or silvery beige when dried.

Good tall subjects 76cm to 152cm (2½ to 5ft) that give striking globes or umbels to dry are the great herbs—the rounded heads of Angelica, Dill, Fennel and Lovage.

From the vegetable garden use the beautiful Allium flowers and seed heads (Chives, Onion and Leeks). Gather the seed heads when they are swollen and almost touching each other.

Top The brightly coloured seed heads of autumn, such as these rose hips, can be preserved in a variety of ways. Varnish can be painted on or even linseed oil can be rubbed in to give a gloss finish.

Above left Moluccella laevis (Bells of Ireland) can be used fresh or dried in flower arrangements. It has tiny shell-like flowers with bell-like sheaths, growing in attractive whorls and spirals around the stem, turning silvery-grey when dried.

Above right The beautiful lanterns of Physalis franchetti formed around its berries. Collect when the first lanterns are turning orange and allow to dry.

Right A decorative relation of the onion, Allium albopilosum, makes a splendid addition to flower arrangements.

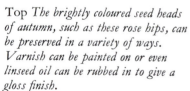

A selection of some of the seed heads and leaves to find or buy for use in dried arrangements. Shown clockwise from left to right *fern (bleached), Cyprus palm, South African lily, Wheat, Lotus, Poppy head, Pine cones, Thistle head, Wood Lotus,* and *Protea,* with *Sweet Corn* in the centre of the picture.

Gourds

Curcubita pepo (Gourds), sometimes referred to as Pumpkins in seed catalogues, are usually grown only for decoration. Some are edible but not particularly tasty, while others are definitely unsuitable for human consumption.

Gourds belong to the Cucumber family and are easily grown from seed sown in the spring in a box containing seed sowing compost. When the seedlings are about 5cm (2in) high transfer each one carefully. Plant each one in its own 10 to 15cm (4 to 6in) pot or in a garden in a rich warm soil. The trailing plants need plenty of water and liquid

Below *A basket of gourds showing some of the shapes that can be grown. Even in a simple basket, the gourds make a charming feature.*

Left *Ornamental gourds produce fruit of widely varying shapes and sizes. Many varieties bear warts or scars.* Below far left *Another member of the same family, a pumpkin can also be grown simply for decorative purposes.* Below left *Gourds wired up and used in an arrangement. For a glossy finish, they should be rubbed with linseed oil or varnished.*

fertilizer, and it is wise to tie the stem up a trellis or strings. Outdoors, support the developing fruits on pieces of wood or slate to prevent slug and moisture damage.

Gourds are usually ripe for picking in the autumn. There are two ways of drying them. Cut them with 10cm (4in) stems attached, tie string and hang from a beam or nails in a warm airy place.

Alternatively, place the gourds on a wooden tray in a warm room, turning them over from time to time. They will ripen completely in about 14 to 21 days, becoming much lighter in weight and ready for decorative purposes and arrangements.

To give the fruits a glossy appearance rub them with linseed oil or varnish. For a high gloss, paint them with clear varnish. This treatment is also suitable for seed heads.

From a packet of mixed ornamental Gourd seeds you will get a number of fruits of various shapes, which can look like marrows [squash], cucumbers, apples, pears, pumpkins and flattened melons. Size will vary considerably and colour will range from pale yellow to dark green, orange and white; often the colours are mixed in curious markings.

Some gourds have warty skins, which add to their textural interest. It is also possible to obtain from certain seedsmen packets of seeds of individual species: apple-shaped (pale striped cream), Turban (orange-red, white of yellow flattened 'marrows'), pear-shaped (green and yellow striped), and small pimply hybrids (apple-shaped with multicoloured, very bumpy skins).

Grasses

You can start collecting grasses quite early in the summer, as they become fully mature, so that they do not shed seeds. In a whole flower arrangement, grass stems can be used for mounting flower heads and leaves, as their flexible stems fall into soft curves quite naturally.

There is a wide selection of ornamental grasses available, and they can easily be grown from seed. One word of warning—many of these set seed easily so grow them by themselves. They can be used on their own or mixed with dried flowers to create original decorations. Here is a list of grasses suitable for preserving:

Agrostis nebulosa (cloud grass) grows to 46cm (18in) and has a charming head like a cloud of tiny flowers.

Briza maxima (pearl grass) [big quaking grass] and *Briza media* (perennial quaking grass) have little hanging pendants nodding in the breeze. They grow to 46cm (18in) and dry very well.

Coix lacryma-jobi (Job's tears) reaches 61 to 91·5cm (24 to 36in) and has pea-sized

Below *Agrostis nebulosa* (*cloud grass*) *is one of the most graceful of all flowering grasses with its soft feathery flowers. They should be cut before they are fully open to prevent them shedding seeds.*
Below right *Hordeum jubatum, an annual, is grown in the garden solely for its decorative feathery flowerheads.*

Above left *Briza maxima (Pearl grass) with its dainty pendulous heads.*
Left *The white and downy heads of lagurus ovatus (hare grass).*
Below *Eragrostis (Love grass) is a hardy annual with graceful feathery inflorescences.*

Above *The large silvery plumes of*
Cortaderia Argentea (Pampas grass).

seeds of pearly grey-green (which can be strung as beads) and thick leaves like maize.

Eragrostis elegans (love grass) has been beautiful panicles (loose irregular arrangement of flowerheads) of cloudy florets, and grows to 61 to 91·5cm (24 to 36in).

Festuca ovina glauca (sheep's fescue) [blue fescue] is a blue tufted grass with pretty small spikes of flowers. This is one of the shorter grasses, rarely exceeding a height of 15cm (6in).

Hordeum jubatum (squirrel tail grass) [foxtail barley] grows up to 61cm (24in) and

has feathery silver-grey flower heads on spiky wiry stems. Cut this young or the tails will disintegrate.

Lagurus ovatus (hare's tail) with its strong stems and fluffy, silky soft heads can be used fresh or dry.

Triticum spelta (ornamental wheat) [Timopheeri] is very decorative with a name that speaks for itself.

There are many more grasses, some perennial, from the well-known Wheat, Barley, Oats and Millet right up to the giant 3·1m (10ft) tall Cortaderia Argentea (Pampas grass) with its silvery plumes.

Foliage

The early autumn foliage of deciduous trees such as Oak, Elm, Beech, Lime and Eucalyptus can all be preserved but do not leave it too late before picking them as you are in danger of the leaves falling—leaving you the proud possessor of a jar of bare winter twigs. Most evergreens such as Holly, Spruce and Bay will dry green on their own, although they do have a shorter life than other dried materials.

Ferns turn brown when they are dried. Gather the young fronds that have not started to curl and particularly avoid those with brown spores on their undersides as they do not dry well. Ferns will retain their colour best if pressed between sheets of newspaper.

It is really well worth remembering *Senecio Maritima* and *Senecio Laxifolius* when thinking of foliage. They both retain their grey leaf colouring well when dried—this looks good in most arrangements and makes a pleasant change from the usual copper and bronze leaf tints which can sometimes seem synonymous with dried foliage arrangements.

Left *Choisya leaves can be pressed and used in both dried flower arrangements or in pressed decorations. They can also be glycerined and bleached for a more decorative effect.*

Below *Evergreens, such as this variegated holly leaf, should be washed thoroughly then pressed lightly to preserve its shape and colour.*

Drying and preserving

There are three basic ways of preserving plant material such as flowers, foliage, seed heads, leaves and grasses. Try them all if you can. If you can't, choose the method most suited to the facilities that you have available.

Air-drying If, for example, you have an airy space with room for hooks or a line to hang the flowers on, then try the air-drying method.

Pressing Some plant material, especially ferns and leaves will retain their colour and shape particularly well if treated in this way.

Dessicant powder Flowers dried out by this method—in a dessicant powder such as borax or silica gel—may be easier for some in that the only space required is a large box to hold the powder and the flowers.

Glycerine Plant material can be preserved with glycerine; the main requirements are some jars, bottles and the space to store them upright.

Gathering flowers

Remember to cut the flowers on a dry, warm day when there will be a minimum of moisture on the plant surface. Never pick material when it is raining or when dew is forming. As a general rule, choose flowers just before they come to full bloom. Fully opened blossoms, or flowers that have already begun to set seed, will merely shed petals and seeds as you attempt to preserve them.

Air drying

Pick the material and remove the leaves from the stems. Leaves that are left on will simply wither and tangle on the stems as they are drying.

If the flowers are fairly small, put them into small bunches and tie them with string or plastic ties, leaving a loop to slide on to a line or hook.

If you have chosen material with large flower heads, try to hang them separately. There is nothing more frustrating than to dry flowers perfectly and then to damage them in trying to disentangle the florets. As the material dries it will tend to shrink, so you may need to tighten the ties to hold the stems securely.

The bunches must be hung, well apart, on a line or on hooks in a cool, dry, airy and dark place. Too much light and warmth tends to make the material brittle and faded, and flowers become mildewed in damp surroundings.

Flowers with heavy or fragile heads can be dried by standing them upright in a jar. For this method make sure that the plant has a strong stem and that the head does not tend to droop. If the stems are very short, immediately after picking cut them down to about 2·5 cm (1in) from the head and push a length of 0·9cm (19 to 20 gauge) florists' wire up the stem and into the flower head and push the end of the wire into a bed of sand or a piece of plastic foam. Leave the flowers to dry in this position.

The length of drying time necessary varies enormously. Delicate material such as grasses may only take a week, but heavier flowers, containing more moisture, may need three weeks or more.

The material should be checked to see if it feels quite dry before removing it for storage.

Hydrangea and molucella, both very popular in dried flower arrangements require a little extra attention. The plants should be cut and stripped of leaves as usual. The stems should then be placed in about 5cm (2in) of water and left in a warm room. When all the water has gone the stems should be tied, hung and left to dry as usual. (Cut hydrangeas on a new stem if possible.)

A list of materials suitable for drying is shown on page 28. This list of plants

Right *The simplest method of drying flowers is the air drying method. The stems should be tied firmly then hung upside down in a dry, airy and dark place. It is always best to disentangle the stems and leaves first to prevent brittle material breaking after they have dried.*

Opposite page above *Drying flowers using a dessicant powder.* 1 *Pour the desiccant powder into a box.* 2 *Place the blossoms carefully in the powder.* 3 *Cover the flowers completely. Leave small flowers for one to two days before testing to see if they are ready. Larger flowers may well take more than a week.*

Opposite page below *A beautifully life-like arrangement using flowers preserved in a dessicant powder.*

is very far from being complete, but it is a guide to suitable material. If you would like to try drying a flower that is not included then there is nothing to lose in experimenting to see if it will work.

Pressing

Evergreens should be treated in a slightly different way. First clean them by washing the leaves in lukewarm water to which a little detergent has been added and then rinsing them, shaking them gently, and leaving them in an airy place. When they are dry, lay them between sheets of newspaper in layers one on top of the other, with a buffer of newspaper or a thick paper towel between each layer. Tie all the layers into a parcel, protecting the top and

Air drying

Varieties	Comments
Rounded shapes Ammobium alatum grandiflorum (Everlasting sand flower)	Stems short in proportion to flower heads so may need lengthening
Anaphalis (Pearl everlasting)	
Helichrysum bracteatum (Straw flower)	Must be cut before flowers are fully opened
Achillea filipendulina (Garden yarrow)	Dry by standing in a jar of water when cut until water evaporates
Catananche caerula (Cupid's dart)	Gather when fully developed
Spiky shapes Acanthus spinosus (Bear's breeches)	Gather when lower florets are at their best. Useful for large arrangements
Delphinium	Pick as soon as top floret opens and dry hanging upside down
Limonium sinuatum (Sea lavender)	Air dry when florets are fully open
Clusters Acacia dealbata (mimosa)	Yellow balls remain and hold some of their perfume.
Eryngium (Sea holly)	Cut before seedheads mature.
Gypsophila elegans (Baby's breath)	Place in a little water and allow to air dry naturally. Also presses well.
Leaves and grasses Aspidistra (Parlour palm)	
Briza maxima (Pearl grass)	
Lagurus ovatus (Hare's tail)	
Seedheads Alliums	Dry upside down
Aquilegia (Columbine)	
Dipsacus fullorium (Teasels)	
Lunaria (Honesty)	Gather when pods begin to change colour

Drying in powder

Varieties	Comments
	Process suits flowers rather than foliage. Simple and open faced flowers are best.
Anemones	
Marigolds	
Daisies	
Cornflowers	
Small roses	Can be very successful if you make sure that the powder is well distributed among the petals

Preserving in glycerine

Varieties	Comments
Clematis vitalba (wild clematis)	Flower heads do not disintegrate and leaves turn deep bronze
Hydrangea	
Molucella laevis (Bells of Ireland)	Preserve in dry place to avoid mould. The mixture may not reach upper flowers so remove a few top flowers before you begin
Convallaria majalis (Lily of the Valley)	Leaves may be completely submerged in the mixture
Fagus sylvatica (Beech)	Pick while still green and fresh. Beech nuts left on the branch will also be preserved
Helleborus (Christmas Rose)	Although these flowers preserve well, they absorb the moisture from the atmosphere and wilt if left in an arrangement for too long.
Magnolia grandiflora (Magnolia)	

bottom with a sheet of cardboard. Put a light weight on top and leave for about a month during which time the leaves will dry. This method stops the branches looking too flat but if you do want them flat simply weight down each single layer with bricks, books, scale-weights or anything handy.

Ferns, too, are perhaps best pressed flat in this way. (They turn brown when dried.)

Drying flowers in powder

The powders used in this method are borax, silica gel crystals, or sand and of these silica gel is probably the best. It dries flowers efficiently and the crystals are very light and therefore less likely to crush delicate blossoms. Furthermore, silica gel crystals can be dried out in a warm oven after use and then used again. Both silica gel and borax can be bought in pharmacies.

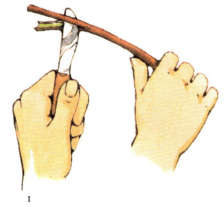

1

2

3

4

The advantage of drying in powder is that flowers preserved by this method retain much of their original colour. Some silica gel preparations on the market have additional chemicals which help retain vivid hues to a truly amazing degree. But these flowers are susceptible to damp and if your room is not fairly dry they should be kept under glass.

Before beginning to use a dessicant powder, the flowers must be dry and in good condition. Any of the powders may be used, although sand tends to be rather heavy for delicate petals.

Cover the bottom of a box or biscuit [cookie] tin with the powder, carefully lay the flowers on this and pour over more of the powder so they are completely covered. Take care that there is plenty of powder between the petals and stamens. Leave them, and the powder will draw the moisture from the petals. Make sure that you do not add any moisture to the mixture by putting the box in a damp place. The box should be kept in a warm dry place.

The length of time it takes to dry the flowers again varies. To test, gently scrape off powder from a petal; if any trace of moisture remains, re-cover and leave. Most small flowers such as violas take about two days to dry completely. Larger flowers, such as dahlias and roses will take six to seven days.

When they are dry, remove and store them in a dark place. Store them in a box, adding a few crystals of silica gel to absorb any moisture.

Florists' wire to support the stems must be added before drying. (For methods of mounting with florists' wire, see page 32).

Materials to choose for powder drying are listed on page 28. The more simple and open-faced flowers really take to this process best.

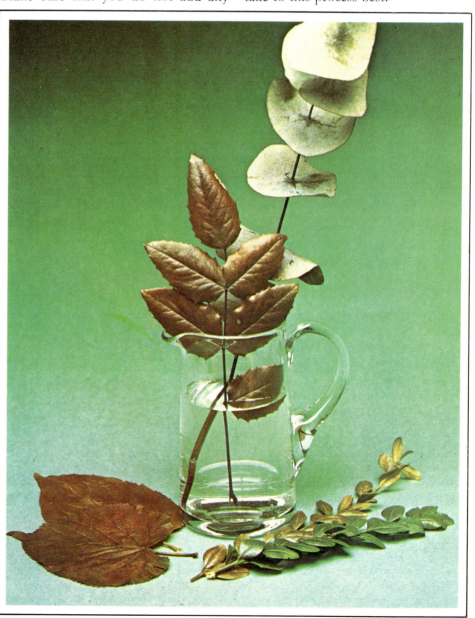

Left *Leaves preserved in glycerine will often undergo a colour change not unattractive in arrangement. Teasel, Clematis, Achillea, Acer and Iris have been added to this arrangement of preserved foliage.*
Below left *A beautiful arrangement of dried leaves, seed heads and fruit.*

Preserving in glycerine

This process replaces the water in the plant with glycerine, giving a supple and long lasting result. Glycerine looks like a clear, syrupy liquid.

Stems should be placed in water for a few hours before putting them in the glycerine. Make sure that the material is in good condition before you begin—attempting to preserve, damaged leaves is a waste of effort. Woody stems should be split to make sure that the glycerine can travel up them.

Make a mixture of two-parts boiling water to one-part glycerine and when cool place the stems in about 10cm (4in) of the liquid. Depending on the type of leaf being glycerined, the time necessary varies between two days to three weeks. The leaves should become supple and change colour. Remove from the glycerine mixture and, if the leaves begin to droop, hang them up-side down for a few days to make sure that the glycerine reaches the top.

Plant material to be preserved by this method should be gathered before the dying autumn colours begin to show—if you leave it too late, the plant loses its power to absorb liquid.

Materials to choose for preserving in glycerine are shown in the table on page 28.

Opposite page *The process of preserving with a glycerine mixture involves replacing the water in the stems with glycerine making the materials much more supple.*
Fig 1 *With woody stems, split them for about 5cm (2in).*
Fig 2 *Stand the branches in a bucket of warm water for a few hours. If any leaves curl up, throw them away as they will not preserve well.*
Fig 3 *Pour the glycerine solution into a narrow container and stand the stems in about 10cm (4in) of the mixture.*
Fig 4 *Put the container into an empty bucket. Allow the branches to soak up the glycerine. The time involved depends upon the type of leaf being glycerined.*

Adapting dried materials

Wiring flowers

The stems of many of the everlasting flowers, and flowers that can be preserved in a drying agent, dry well, but with a rigidity that has limited use in arrangements requiring a soft curving line or a more malleable stem.

To overcome this problem, a false stem can be made with florists' wires. These are usually available in bundles of twenty from florists or garden centres.

It is essential to insert these wires before the flowers are dried. Pick the

1 Insert wire through hollow or soft stem.

2 If stem is woody, push wire into base of flower beside natural stem.

3 Bind false stem to the natural stem with rose wire.

4 Cover with tape.

5 Making a cluster of flowers. Insert wire through the front of flowers.

6 Bind all stems tightly with rose or thin copper wire.

7 To complete, work all round, bending each flower outwards.

8 Making a spike of flowers.

9 Continue adding flowers until the spike reaches the required length.

10 Wiring small preserved leaves.

11 Supporting a large or broad leaf.

flower with 2·5cm (1in) of stem. If the stem is hollow or soft, push the wire through the stem and into the base or receptacle of the flower, being careful not to allow the wire to penetrate through to the front (Fig 1). If the flower has a hardy woody stem, the wire can be inserted into the base, beside the natural stem (Fig 2). Only a short piece of wire need be used at this stage as it can be lengthened later. As the flower dries it shrinks and tightens round the wire, making a firm bond.

To lengthen a stem
To lengthen a false or woody stem, place a piece of wire so that it overlaps the main stem by approximately 2·5cm (1in). Bind together with fine rose wire or thin copper wire (Fig 3). To lengthen a hollow stem, push wire up through the stem and then into the base of the flower.

Binding false stems
To give a more natural appearance to a false stem, it can be bound with gutta-percha tape. This is a plastic self-adhesive tape, obtainable from florists. To bind the stem, take the flower in your right hand and start binding at the top of the stem. Twist the tape around the stem between thumb and forefinger, and with the left hand hold the tape taut while guiding it down to the bottom of the stem (Fig 4).

To make a cluster of flowers
Small flowers such as Gomphrena or Rhodanthe are most suitable to use in clusters and so the flowerets need to be wired. Wire when fresh with fine wire, and then allow to dry. To do this insert a loop of wire through the front of the flowers (Fig 5). Gently pull wire just far enough into the centre so that it cannot be seen. Twist the two wires together to form a stem and cut to 6·5cm (2½in).

Make a posy of the flowers by slightly raising them in the centre and using a long florists' wire for the main stem, insert it in the middle of the posy, and bind together very tightly with rose or thin copper wire, and cover with tape (Fig 6). To complete start at the edge of the posy and work all round, bending each flower outwards (Fig 7).

Making a spike of flowers
The flowers used in making a spike must be graded in size, the smallest ones being used at the top. The topmost flower should have a long stem to act as the main stem, the rest of the flowers

should have stems of about 7·5cm (3in). Guttapercha binding tape is used to hold the flowers in place.

Start binding the long stem as in Fig 4 when 2·5cm (1in) of stem has been bound, place the head of the second flower just under that of the first flower and bind the two stems together (Fig 8).

Continue adding flowers until the spike reaches the required length (Fig 9).

Wiring leaves
Small preserved leaves that need support or a longer stem, need only a single piece of wire laid along the centre back and held in position with clear sticky tape [cellophane] (Fig 10).

To support a larger or broader leaf, make a loop of wire and hold in position with tape (Fig 11).

Skeletonizing leaves
A skeletonized leaf is one which has had all the soft green vegetable matter removed, either naturally or artificially, leaving a cobweb-like structure of veins. They make beautiful and delicate additions to both formal and informal arrangements particularly those used for Christmas table decorations.

The removal of the green matter occurs naturally when the leaves fall to the ground to be eaten by insects, or rotted by the elements. The skeletons of these leaves can sometimes be found under trees and shrubs but, unfortunately, they are often damaged and of little use. Better results can be achieved by hastening the decay. This too has its disadvantages as the rotting material can give off an unpleasant odour.

The method
Place a number of selected leaves into a pan of water that has had a handful of washing soda added to it. Gently simmer for one to two hours and allow to cool.

The green matter should then be soft enough to be removed by scraping with the fingers or a knife, under cold running water. This should be done very carefully so as not to damage the veins. Test one leaf first to see if it has softened sufficiently and, if not, return the pan to the heat and simmer for a little longer.

Finally, rinse the skeleton thoroughly and dry between sheets of blotting paper or soft kitchen paper.

The leaves are usually a dull shade of brown at this stage, but if a paler colour is needed, they can be lightened by

Below The delicate tracery of leaf veins obtained by removing the soft green matter carefully. The skeletonized leaves can then be bleached in a mild solution and used in arrangement.

leaving them in a solution of domestic bleach and water (one tablespoon to one pint of water) for twelve hours. Rinse and dry them carefully.

Most leaves with strong woody veins are suitable for this kind of treatment but Magnolia, Rhododendrons, Laurel and Holly are particularly successful subject.

Dyeing grasses

Dyeing grasses by the method used in florists' shops can be a messy and un-rewarding experience. However, there are other ways that take little trouble and give just as good, if not better, results. The grasses do not develop the sharp, bright hue that you see in shop windows but take on a more delicate, natural colour that mixes well in flower arrangements.

Using food colouring

The basic solution is a mixture of 1 tablespoon of dye to 112g (4 ozs) of water. Some grasses when cut fresh and placed in the dye, will absorb the mixture and take on a soft shade of the colour being used. This coloration will last for a very long time.

This method, however, is not a very reliable one as some stems readily take up the dye while others stubbornly remain green—even stems taken from the same clump of grass will react differently. But there is nothing to lose by trying to get them to drink up the dye first. If this method fails, simply turn them round and submerge their heads into the dye and leave for several hours. Dry by the air drying method or on several sheets of newspaper. If the grass to be dyed is already dry, then the latter method only can be used.

Multi-purpose dyes

Mix the multi-purpose dye as instructed on the label. The amount of dye mixed will depend on the quantity of grasses to be dyed. If the packaging is opened carefully and a small amount of powder removed, it can then be sealed up again with some sticky [cellophane] tape, for future use.

The dye, when mixed, can be kept for a limited period in a screw top jar. Using an old cooking pot, simmer the dye on the stove, then holding the grasses to be dyed in this colour by the stalks, immerse the heads for a minute in the simmering dye. The grasses will quickly take on the colour. Turn the grasses about giving each grass head a chance to be dyed evenly and then dry on several sheets of newspaper.

Grasses and some flowers can be easily dyed in the home by either using a food colourant or a multi-purpose dye. The colours are perhaps not as bright as shop-bought grasses but they often take on a more delicate hue not out of place in dried flower arrangements.

Dried flower arrangements

There are many and varied ways of using dried flowers in the home not least of all in dried flower arrangements. These can be approached in much the same way as fresh flower arrangements —but there are some advantages. Since dried flowers do not require water, it is not necessary for all the stems to stand in a vase—other supports can be used. Also, they are more obedient to the arranger and will not twist and droop in an arrangement. Best of all, dried arrangements are everlasting and so make splendid decorations all year round, especially in the winter when fresh flowers are hard to get and very expensive.

Preparing the material

Before you begin an arrangement, some of the dried plant material may require extra care.

Dried flowers and grasses can also be bought from time to time in florist shops. Florists' stubb wires should be used for making false stems when necessary. The thickness of the wire used depends on the material and its purpose. Gauges 0·90mm, 0·71mm and 0·56mm are the most commonly used. Delicate leaves can be supported with stubb wire, and wire stems concealed with florist's tape (guttapercha). These are available from floral supply houses or can sometimes be purchased from your local florist shop. A hollow corn stalk can be slipped over the wire to conceal it too.

For detailed information on wiring different flowers, see page 32.

It will help to preserve delicate seed heads if you spray them with hair lacquer before arranging them, and many berries can be preserved by brushing them with a mixture of $\frac{1}{2}$ clear shellac and $\frac{1}{2}$ alcohol. Leave them in an airy place to dry.

Supports in the container

Wire mesh The most commonly used support for dried and fresh flowers is crumpled wire mesh with 5cm (2in) gaps. This does not always produce a close enough texture, however, to hold the fine wire stems on some dried material.

Florist's foam such as 'Oasis' (used dry), and blocks of dry foam which are made especially for dried arrangements, are alternatives. As the foam is light and will overbalance easily, it must be anchored to the container. This can be done by impaling it on a pin holder (preferably an Oasis pinholder rather than an ordinary one) by covering it with wire mesh and securing the mesh to the container with a wire, or by wrapping a weight into the base of the foam.

Plasticine can also be used. A lump of this should be pressed firmly into the base of a dry, clean container, and the stems pushed into it. **Plaster of Paris** may be used in the same way provided you can make up your arrangement before it sets hard.

A detergent mix is not only cheaper but sets much less rapidly, giving at least one hour for arranging before setting hard. It also has an added advantage in the fact it can be recycled. To make the mix, add two tablespoons of water to one large cup of detergent.

In all methods it is easier to see what you are doing if you use a shallow container.

Glaring white plaster can be concealed by painting it or rubbing it with brown shoe polish when it is quite dry.

Containers

There are no hard or fast rules about what containers to use for dried arrangements. Glass containers would obviously be unsuitable if you have lots of foam and underpinnings to conceal, but gently curving, golden stems of corn would add to the grace of an arrangement.

Because the containers do not need to be watertight, rush or wicker baskets can be used. A flat wooden slab makes

Opposite page An informal display of autumnal seedheads and dried grasses. Dried flower arrangements should be approached in much the same way as for fresh flowers but they are more obedient to the arranger and will not twist and droop.

an excellent base, using well-disguised plasticine as a support. Smaller arrangements can be made to fit snugly into a scallop shell or a candlestick. Candles themselves look pretty surrounded by dried flowers, but be very careful to keep the dried material well away from the flame as it is highly inflammable.

Arranging the material

It is most likely that if you care enough about flowers to make the effort to select and preserve them, you will also have a feeling for making them look attractive in an arrangement.

Assuming you have chosen a con-

tainer and have the necessary supports firmly in place, then the next step is to arrange your material.

A good rule is to have different quantities of the various flowers or leaves.

Remember, various colours, textures and shapes make for more interesting arrangements.

Your arrangements can be as delicate or as elaborate as you wish—a few wispy flowers in muted tones on a coffee table make an effective 'shape', or a straight forward, formal arrangement, made very much as though you were working with fresh flowers and bearing in mind each flower's contribution to

Below *A formal arrangement showing how dried flowers and leaves can be used in the same way as fresh flowers. The outline points of the triangle are fixed in position first (Fig 1) and the filler material is then arranged around them (Fig 2).*

Below right *A simple but delicate arrangement using the flower heads of grasses together with the seed heads of Honesty and the poppy.*

the whole arrangement. Alternatively you can make a fabulous massed concoction. By adding new sprigs, even green ones, and letting them dry in the arrangement, it becomes an ever-growing one. This kind of arrangement is entirely dependent on your materials, how much space there is in the room and the size of your container.

For the more traditional arrangement, however, you need to follow a basic building procedure.

Formal arrangements need a basic outline, focal interest and filling material. The first step is to place the tall outline material. Place the first three

pieces to fix the outline points—make the three points of a triangle, for example, with the stems coming from a central point. To give depth to the arrangement, avoid putting the outline points on the same plane.

The items which make up the focal points of the arrangement should be placed near the middle and fairly low in the overall pattern. Don't make this part so strong that it kills the rest of the material, add just enough material to make the arrangement come to life. Hydrangea or clusters of vivid berries would be a good choice for this position. Filler material—grasses for exam-

1   2

ple—should be used to blend the focal interest points with the outline material. The aim is not to fill in all the remaining gaps but to make the whole arrangement harmonize. This is a dangerous stage in the arrangement, when it is very tempting to go on adding more and more material. Stop when you see that there is enough material to complete a graceful design.

Re-using

Dried flowers can be reused indefinitely in arrangements of different sizes, com-

binations and shapes, provided they are treated with special care. Glycerined material can be wiped over with a damp cloth, and dust can be removed from dried material with a soft sable brush. Some are, of course, more brittle than others, and all are liable to break. It is not unusual, however, to keep on using the same flowers in different arrangements for years, and they can be stored away in the attic or a cupboard [closet] when not in use, during the summer when the scents of freshly cut flowers make them an irresistible change.

Below *The orange heads of dried sweet corn form the focal point of this arrangement of bleached ferns and seedheads.*
Opposite page *Dried stems and heads of giant Hogweed in a cylindrical glass vase make a permanent and elegant arrangement.*

Left *A formal arrangement of flowers giving emphasis to the light and delicate colours of dried flowers. The whole arrangement is based on a triangle formation and is then filled in with a mass of bright and colourful materials.*

Left *Mixing both dried and fresh materials can result in a successful arrangement of bright colours and interesting textural shape. Where dried flowers are to be used with water, it is probably best if the stems are wired first to prevent them rotting away in the container.*

Right *A magnificent, massed arrangement by David Hicks is evergrowing as well as being everlasting. It is built up by continually adding fresh sprigs that are then allowed to dry in the arrangement. The materials used include bullrushes, pampas grass, box, hemlock and oak.*

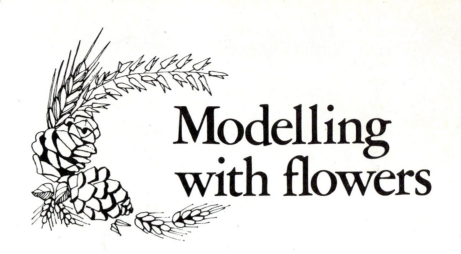

Modelling with flowers

There are many novel and decorative ways of using dried flowers, other than in making flower arrangements. You can use them to decorate all sorts of small corners throughout the house—for instance, binding them into posies, decorating Chinese soup spoons and bowls, or making hanging flower balls or as a dried flower candle base.

Styrofoam is the basis of many decorations. It is available from most craft shops and comes in many shapes and sizes—from ball and egg shapes to domes, cones and discs, logs, pedestals and pyramids. Similar in texture to polystyrene, it is ideal for dried flower decorations as it does not flake or crumble.

To make a flower ball
Flower balls make excellent gifts and bazaar items; being cheap, simple and quick to make.

You will need a styrofoam ball to use as a base. The flower ball illustrated on the opposite page has been made up using Helichrysum bracteatum in a variety of colours, but any dried flowers can be used depending upon the size of your base.

Left Some of the many delightful ways of using dried flowers. Small posies can be made up by wiring the stems and then covering them with decorative tape; Chinese soup spoons can be used as miniature containers, and the base of a candle can be given a delightful finish by surrounding it with a mass of tiny flower heads interspersed with larger varieties.

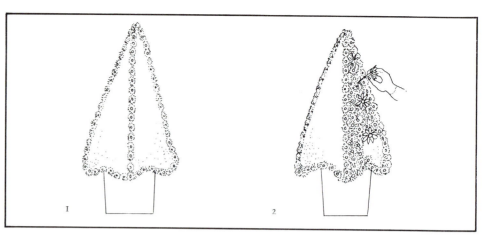

Below *Flower trees are quite simple to make. Cut the foam to the shape you require and place the flowers to give a basic outline to your design* (Fig 1) *Then simply fill in the rest of the tree with a mass of flowers* (Fig 2). *The tiny basket is made by covering the handle with delicate flower heads stuck down with a rubber-based adhesive [rubber cement]. The basket is then filled with a delightful mixture of flowers and grasses.*

1

2

Cut the flower stalks off close to the head and then simply pin each flower directly onto the ball, ensuring that the pin head is concealed. Continue until the ball is completely covered and none of the foam shows through. Then simply pin on a loop of velvet ribbon with which to hang it up or place it on a dressing table for a sweet reminder of summer.

To make the flower trees
You can either use one of the many styrofoam shapes available or adapt one by cutting it to the required shape.

Position the flowers to give an outline to the tree, then fill in with dried flowers. If the stems of the flowers are not strong enough, then the flower heads only should be pinned on.

To make the basket
Choose a basket of the required shape and size and sew or stick a piece of ribbon around the edge. Choose a number of small flowers for the handle, remove their stems and stick down gently using a rubber-based adhesive. Then simply fill up the basket with brightly coloured flowers.

Left A simple bay tree is an example of some of the fanciful trees in all sizes which can be made by sticking materials into a foam ball. Find a pot or tub the right size to plant your tree in and then place a few heavy pebbles in the bottom. If it is a large pot, fill to about 2·5cm (1in) below the rim with stones and cover with plaster and cement.

Place a thin rod in the centre and allow it to set in the plaster. The length of the rod should be in proportion to the size of the pot. Make sure the rod stays vertical while the filler dries, propping it up if necessary. When the plaster is dry, it can be disguised by placing pebbles on top or by painting it.

Take a ball of foam and push it down over the rod until it is embedded about half way. The size of the ball again is a matter of personal choice. A general rule is to choose a ball about half the size of the pot.

Wind a piece of string tightly around the rod at the base of the ball to prevent the foam slipping further down the rod. The string will be concealed by the dried material—or can be disguised by tying a strip of ribbon over it.

At this point it is a good idea to paint the rod and pot to harmonize with the arrangement.

Add the material to the ball starting from the top. Keep all the dried material to a stem length of not more than 5cm (2in) and if necessary mount on stub wires. Use your largest material first, pushing it closely into the surface before adding the smaller flowers and grasses.

47

Left *This enchanting pendant decoration is made by using a ball of styrofoam as a base.*
You will also need a collection of dried flower heads, artificial cherries, pine cones, husks, dried leaves and grasses. Cut a length of wire, sufficient to pass through the plastic ball, with a hook at one end and a loop at the other. Push the wire through the ball so that the hook holds it in place.
Tie a ribbon bow through the loop of the wire, leaving a long strip for hanging. Cut the flower stems slantwise to make sure they are firmly held and push into the ball. Twist florists' wire around the weaker stems to strengthen them and work around the ball until all the foam is covered.

Right *For this candle base you will need either a styrofoam base to fit the size of your container or a short length of fine mesh wire. The wire will then have to be crumpled up and formed into a circular shape to fit the container. Place your candle in the centre firmly then simply thread your flowers into the arrangement.*
One word of warning: Do not allow the candle to burn down too low as dried materials will catch fire very easily.

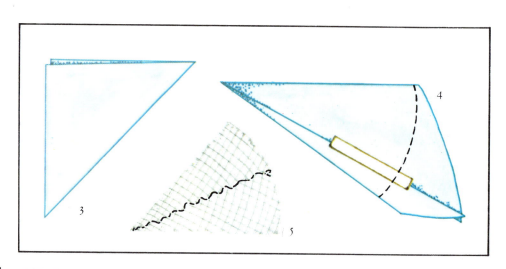

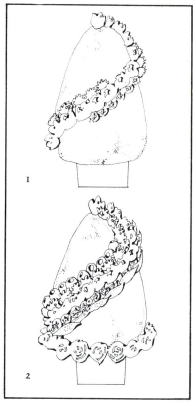

Seed heads provide textural interest to a cone arrangement. All these objects can be found whilst beachcombing or whilst out for a country walk.

This spiral design is arranged on a foam cone but larger designs often benefit from being worked on a wire cone (see opposite).

Gather your materials together first and try to work out exactly how the materials can be used. If you have no stems on the seed heads, it is best if you wire them to the appropriate length first. The shorter lengths should be placed in the top and the longer lengths, to be concealed by your other materials, should fall at the bottom. Having worked out your design, find the central spiral (Fig 1). Work this first and then fill in the design from this central point (Fig 2).

Many larger designs will need a cone
base larger and more stable than those
available in the shops. A wire mesh
base is both practical to make and can
be made to fit the size of the design
you choose to make.

For this you will need: Newspaper
or other paper for a pattern.
Wire mesh with 1·2cm (½in) holes
for the cone.
Wire cutters or floral scissors.
Fine wire or twine for binding the
edges together.
Crumbled florists' foam.
Masking or adhesive tape.

Make the pattern from a piece of
paper by folding a square shape in half
to make a triangle (Fig 3).
Join the two short sides with a piece
of tape so that they form a cone shape,
and trim the base evenly so it can stand
upright (Fig 4). Then cut the tape
and stretch out the pattern over the
wire mesh. Cut around the pattern
with shears and join the edges of the
wire by binding them with fine wire or
twine (Fig 5).
Line the inside of the cone with the
newspaper pattern and fill the interior
with crumbled foam, packing it tightly.
Seal off the base of the cone by putting
overlapping strips of tape across it,
preferably making two layers—the
second at right angles to the first.

Right A fir cone tree made of natural
and bleached fir cones. Cones can be
bleached by soaking them for a short
period of time in a strong household
bleach. It is important to work in
rubber gloves and preferably outdoors
as the fumes of the bleach are very
strong. Place your materials into the
solution and leave for a few minutes.
If the bleach is strong enough, the
materials will change colour
immediately.
When they are as light as you require,
remove them and dry in front of a fan
heater, otherwise the cones will close up.
For ferns and leaves a weaker solution
of bleach is used. Take care not to
leave the skeletons in the solution too
long as the bleach will eventually make
the leaves disintegrate. Dry the leaves
gently and either press flat between
two sheets of blotting paper or allow
to curl.

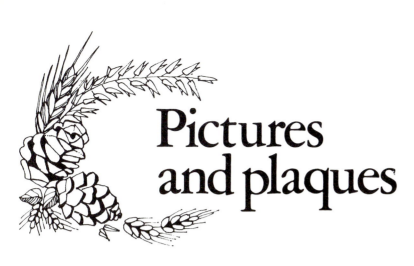

Pictures and plaques

Making a flower picture is one of the most delightful ways of displaying the materials that you have gathered and preserved. Plaques can be any size or shape and covered with a variety of fabrics, thus giving a lot of scope for interesting designs and unusual effects. Putting flowers under glass, is a permanent way of keeping them looking fresh and colourful, and, being protected from dust, they will last for many years.

Choosing a frame

A frame is not always necessary for mounting a dried flower picture, as a plaque or wood block can set off a design just as well. However, a frame with a glass front can be useful to give a more formal aspect to the picture.

As preserved flowers do not naturally lie flat, it is essential to have a frame with a deep recess between the glass and the backing. Searching junk shops can often reveal just such a frame with a curved glass front, making an ideal setting for a design. But failing this, an ordinary square or oblong frame with flat glass can be adapted to accommodate the depth of the dried flowers, by sticking or tacking 1·3cm (½in) by 1·3cm (½in) wood beading to the back of the frame, making a box-like structure. A backing for this frame is then cut to fit the outside measurements of the box

One of the main elements of successful design in dried flower pictures is to use the natural shapes of the materials themselves.

Left A bold design using the gently curving lines and darker shades of the leaves to set off the simple lines and autumnal colours of the grass and flower heads.

Below A more gentle effect is achieved by using loosely clustered grass heads and delicately coloured flowers to give a much softer, flowing line to a basic diagonal design.

frame. Cover the backing and the insides of the box with material of your choice. After making your design on the backing, glue firmly onto the frame.

Backing materials

For a picture in a frame, all sorts of materials can be used but those with a natural appearance usually complement everlasting flowers. Materials such as hessian [burlap], cork or wood can be used, although felt and velvet are also used to great effect. For a simple start, plain or coloured card can be used.

Making a plaque

For a plaque the required shape should be cut out of 5 or 9mm ($\frac{1}{4}$ or $\frac{1}{3}$in) plywood. If covering with a backing material, such as velvet, stick it down, using a rubber based adhesive [rubber cement]. Trim the edges then add a braid. Before starting the design ensure that there is a hole for the hanging device in the plaque, as it will be too late once the design has been started.

Making the design

The most important part of making up a design is to study the shape of the flowers themselves, for although you can change their shape slightly, following their natural curves will look best.

Having studied the flowers, attempt a preliminary sketch first, for once you start glueing the flowers into position, it will be too late to change the design without ruining the materials.

Begin placing the flowers on the outside edge of your design first, then work towards the centre, covering any unsightly stems as you proceed.

For a well-balanced design, use small or pointed shapes on the outside and larger flowers in the centre. Use glue sparingly, on the back of the flowers only.

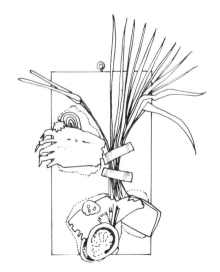

Festive decorations

Everlasting flowers and seedheads are useful for giving the house a festive air. Used in conjunction with other materials, they can provide unusual and interesting decorations for table centrepieces and elsewhere throughout the house for a special occasion.

A table centrepiece

A beautiful table centrepiece can be made from a mixture of evergreens, painted seedheads, fresh Christmas roses, dried flowers and leaves and tree ornaments.

If you have no trough-shaped container, use a shiny bread baking tin. As a holder within the container, large mesh wire-netting will serve if it is crumpled to fit the trough from base to brim. Place the candles in position first then mass short snippets of foliage around their base. Arrange the ornaments on firm drinking straws and, for the sake of the fresh flowers, top up with water.

If the flower arrangement is designed to last for a long time, the stems of the dried materials should be wired to prevent them rotting away in the water.

Decorations under glass

A couple of tall glass jars with plain cork tops and a multitude of fir cones painted in scarlet and bright blue are the materials for these unusual decorations.

Aerosol paints are ideal for the fiddly job of painting the cones. Ensure the whole area in which you are spraying is

Opposite page This splendid trophy is made from a vast array of seemingly disparate objects which with a little time and care can be made into an intricate and fascinating design. The whole design was carefully planned before any work was started. Remember, if you wish to hang the panel, you should put a screw or hook in the board before you begin. The base upon which to build up your design can be either plasticine, clay, filling plaster or a detergent mix—all are equally effective. For stems, sticky tape can be used as it will be hidden by materials added later.
Start with the materials at the back of the design, then build up the structure until the board is hidden and the panel complete.

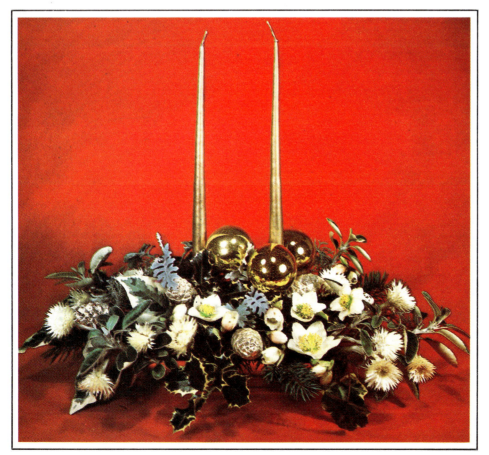

Left An attractive centrepiece for a Christmas table using a mixture of dried and fresh flowers, leaves and painted cones.

covered with newspaper and hold the can at least 10cm (4in) away from the materials. Stand the jars where the light, whether natural or artificial, can shine through them, making the colour sparkle.

A long lasting flower pyramid

A Byzantine cone, made from dried flowers and paper drinking mats [coasters] can be transformed into 'blooms'. The centre of each bloom is an individual flower from the grey-leaved santolina. Thread the flower through the paper circle and fold it into a cone shape. The whole arrangement is based on a foam cone available from florists. A short piece of cane in the base of the cone holds it in the vase. Starting at the top, work downwards, placing each 'bloom' in the cone. Remember that the lower stems must be longer than the top ones.

Opposite page *A beautiful autumnal decoration based around a length of wood.*

To make this design you will need Dried flowers, leaves, dyed grasses, fir cones and plastic fruit (optional). A fairly smooth length of wood (a simple stick will work just as well) measuring about 30·5cm (1ft). Florists' wire A length of ribbon.

Starting at the top of the stick, in this case with barley, bind the material to the stick with florists' wire. Keep adding extra material as you work downwards. The widest part of the design should fall around the middle of the stick. From this point the design should start to taper off. Work until the wood is fully covered then finally wind the ribbon around the centre and finish with a bow.

Centre *Sparkling decorations under glass are simple enough even for children to make. Stand the jars where the light can shine through them making the colour sparkle.*

Left *A long-lasting flower pyramid, based on a basic cone shape, made by combining individual flowers of santolina with folded drinking mats.*

57

Crystallized flowers

Finally, a further method of drying flowers is to crystallize them.

These scented and sparkling flowers make an attractive and long-lasting decoration for later use on iced cakes, desserts and ice-creams or, if packed in a beautiful jar, a delightful and unusual present.

They are simple to make and far more attractive than commercially produced decorations. Choose any flower, except those grown from a bulb, which may be poisonous. Rose, violet, cowslip, primrose, flowering cherry and apple blossom are particularly suitable. Select whole flowers or petals which are fresh and undamaged but never with rain or dew upon them. The gum arabic and rose water may be bought from a pharmacy.

You will need:

15 g (½oz) [½ tablespoon] gum arabic
1 tablespoon rose water
4 small posies of flowers
90 g (3oz) [⅜ cup] castor [superfine] sugar

Place the gum arabic and the rose water in a screw top jar. Put the lid on firmly and shake the jar for two to three minutes. Set the jar aside for one to three hours, shaking it occasionally, or until the gum arabic is dissolved. The length of time depends on the size of the gum arabic pieces. Pour the dissolved gum arabic into a bowl.

Line a backing sheet with grease-proof or waxed paper.

Cut the stalks from the flowers leaving 0·6cm (¼in) near the flower. Hold the flowers by their stalks, and with a soft, fine paint brush, paint the petals on both sides with the dissolved gum arabic.

Place one tablespoon of the sugar on a plate. Using your fingertips or a pair of tweezers, gently dip each flower into the sugar, coating both sides.

As the sugar on the plate becomes damp, discard it, and replace with another tablespoon of sugar.

Place the coated flowers on the lined backing sheet and leave in a warm dry place for at least 24 hours. An airing cupboard [linen closet] is the ideal place, though the flowers will dry out at room temperature (this may take longer). When the flowers are dry and hard, store them in a glass jar with a tight fitting lid.

Below Flowers crystallized in the home are far more attractive than those to be found in the shops and the choice of flowers is much wider. Use them to decorate cakes and sweets or place them in a beautiful glass jar for an unusual present.

The scents of summer

The sweet scents of summer

The fragrances of sweet smelling herbs, spices and flowers can be captured all year round in pot-pourri and sachets. Rooms, cupboards [closets] and personal linen can be kept fragrant and fresh with all the varieties of aromatic plants. You can give each drawer or cupboard a distinctive scent—sweet, spicy, delicate or intoxicating—making it both a special pleasure to open and the contents delightful to wear or use in the home.

Fragrant flowers and herbs grow everywhere. They can be gathered and dried or they can be bought already dried at herbalist shops and mixed at home with essential oils and fixatives to give them scent. It is in the subtle blending of these fragrances and, in pot-pourri, of colour too, that herbal art lies.

Harvesting herbs and flowers

Spring and summer are the seasons to harvest herbs and flowers for sweet-smelling pot-pourri, sachets and herb pillows, for once winter comes most of the herbs vanish from sight.

You must harvest herbs when their aromatic oils are most powerful, so pick them just before they flower, in the early morning when the dew has dried and before the sun is hot. Pick flowers when they are just open and absolutely unblemished, even though it seems hard to plunder them at that moment.

Harvest seeds when they are ready to fall, and roots at the end of the season. Pick only enough to lightly cover whatever drying shelves you have arranged and let the leaves remain on the stem. Separate any petals you want. Handle both leaves and flowers very gently to prevent bruising. As you pick herbs or flowers, lay them one deep on a tray or flat box.

Drying herbs and flowers
Your aim is to dry the herbs quite quickly with an even, low warmth—not less than 21°C (70°F) or more than 38°C (100°F). A good, even ventilation is just as important as the heat to carry away the humidity of the drying plants. Too much heat or too sunny or light a place will brown the leaves or, at least, dissipate the aromatic properties you are trying to conserve. So you want a dark place with little or no dust, but warmth and plenty of air.

Possible drying places are an airing cupboard [linen closet] a warming compartment of an oven, a darkened, warm well-ventilated room, passage [hallway] or cupboard where you could set up a small fan heater; an attic, garage or darkened greenhouse; a dry well-aired cellar, perhaps near a boiler.

The shelves must be well separated so that air can pass freely between them. You could use muslin tacked to a wooden framework, hessian [burlap] or any open weave cloth stretched over dowels or framing, or the flat bottoms of storage boxes which have been perforated to let air through, but do not use wire mesh.

If you can alter and regulate the heat, one method is to begin drying with a temperature of about 32°C (90°F) for one day and then reduce the heat to 21°C (70°F) until the drying process is finished.

The drying space should only faintly smell of herbs; a strong smell means there is too much heat and escaping aromas. Don't add a fresh batch of herbs until the first batch is dry or you will add more humidity to the air. Turn the herbs as they are drying from time to time. Experiment with drying until you get the fullest colour and smell in the herbs.

It takes from four to fourteen days or more to dry herbs and flowers. Some flowers, such as rosemary flowers, are better dried slowly at a lower temperature than herbs.

Leaves are dry when they are brittle but will not shatter. Flower petals should feel dry and slightly crisp. Roots should dry right through with no soft centre. Store all dried plants in airtight containers in a cool, dark place.

Air drying
Tying a bunch of herbs and flowers and hanging them upside down in a dry, airy space is an old method of drying herbs, and more satisfactory in a dry climate than in a humid one. Air drying is likely to retain less colour and scent but needs no special arrangements.

Pot-pourri
Pot-pourri can be made of all scented plants—flowers, fruits, herbs, barks, spices—and it is the blending of these that produces the dimly fragrant, sometimes mysterious, aromas.

Choose a main scent—it is often rose petals in a pot-pourri, lavender in a sachet—then add others to give the mixture fleeting undertones. You can also add drops of essential oils bought from a herb stockist. A fixature such as orris root, is needed to hold the perfumes longer than the flowers and the leaves on their own.

Choose a beautiful container—an apothecary jar, open-work silver or ceramic pot, china or porcelain box or urn. If the pot-pourri is to be seen, arrange it with leaves of elusive greens, small rose buds, marigolds, pressed violets, pansies and everlasting flowers. Some of these do not hold their scent as well, as, say roses, tuberose and lavender, but they give perfect shape and delicate colour.

Experiment with scents because they vary from garden to garden and overlap from plant to plant. For example neroli is a scented substance in fragrant roses which is also in geraniums, jasmine, orange blossom and wallflowers. Citronellol is in roses and eucalyptus, and eugenol is in bay, cloves, hyacinths and tuberoses. The choice of scent is infinite —violet, jonquil, narcissus, lilac, honeysuckle, lily of the valley, the mints, rose geranium, rosemary, and in warm climates, oleander, magnolia, lotus, jasmine, gardenia, orange blossom, acacia or wattle bark.

Also consider using these—cloves, nutmeg, cinnamon, mace, vanilla pod from the Mexican creeper, woodruff, tonquin beans, sandalwood, cedar and sassafras, eucalyptus leaves and citrus peel.

Floral pot-pourri
There are dozens of combinations to experiment with, but this one is simple.
1 lit (2pt) rose petals

Opposite page *Flowers need not be dried solely for their looks—with care their delicate scents can also be preserved and used in a variety of ways. Sachets, pillows and pot-pourri are just a few of the many uses to keep a room or drawer smelling sweet and fresh.*

0·5 lit (1pt) rose geranium leaves
0·5 lit (1pt) lavender flowers
1 cup rosemary needles
2 tablespoons each of ground cloves, cinnamon, allspice
3 tablespoons crushed orris root and powdered gum benzoin
20 drops essential oil of rose
5 drops essential oil of sandalwood or citrus.

Jasmine pot-pourri

0·5 lit (1pt) jasmine flowers
0·3 lit (½pt) orange blossoms and gardenias
0·3 lit (½pt) geranium leaves, including the lemon, peppermint and rose scented ones
57g (2oz) cassia
57g (2 oz) gum benzoin
A vanilla pod or drops of vanilla oil.

Herbal pot-pourri

Choose the leaves from angelica, basil, bay, rose, geranium, bergamot, borage, lemon balm, lemon verbena, thyme or lemon thyme, lovage, marjoram, mint, rosemary, sage, sweet cicely, tarragon and eucalyptus.

Choose flowers from borage, camomile, elder, lavender, lime cowslips, cornflowers, clover, marigolds, nasturtiums, rose petals, wallflowers and violets.

Choose spices from ground cardamom, cinnamon, cloves, nutmeg, citrus peel and coriander.

To make a pot-pourri

Add drops of oils to dried flowers and fixatives, then put flowers, leaves and spices in layers in the container. Use very small, whole flowers and leaves to decorate the top layer. Place mixture in airtight container and leave the jar for six weeks, turning the ingredients weekly.

Herb pillows

For dreams of summer, put a herb pillow in your pillow case. Herbs to soothe the insomniac include angelica, woodruff, sage, hops, dill, camomile, bergamot, lavender, valerian (a rather unpleasant smell), lemon balm, lemon verbena, tarragon, elder flowers and borage.

The herbs that were used for strewing on bare floors in the Middle Ages are also good for herb pillows—thyme, mint, basil, hyssop, marjoram and rosemary.

Make a cotton or muslin bag to any size you want, to hold the herbs, and then make a cover for it that can be laundered in sprigged cotton or perhaps white embroidery on white cotton. Mix together equal parts of lavender, lemon verbena and mint, and add small quantities of any of the herbs listed above.

Or mix equal parts of rosemary blossoms, rosemary needles, pine needles, rose geranium leaves and lemon balm.

Or mix equal parts of rose petals and lavender and add small amounts of woodruff, camomile, dill, sage, bergamot and tarragon. Or use hops only. Many people feel a hop pillow is best for insomnia.

Sachets

Hang these on hangers; put them in drawers, linen cupboards [closets] and under cushions. Try a half and half mixture of lavender and lemon verbena; or southernwood, bergamot and lemon balm with twice as many rose petals and lavender.

If you wish, add to any of these mixtures some spices—coriander seeds, cloves or cinnamon.

Sachets can be made or small squares of silk, cotton print or organdie, and treated as miniature pillows, or they can be gathered across the top and secured with a ribbon. This method means this can be refilled later on.

An orange and clove pomander is easy enough for a child to make and releases a delicious spicy smell to perfume a wardrobe or to keep linen smelling fresh.

To make a pomander you will need
1 orange.
1·4m (1½ yds) brown cord or velvet ribbon
Packets of allspice, cinnamon and whole cloves.
Begin by making channels for the cord using cloves. To form the first horizontal groove, press two parallel lines of cloves right round the orange, leaving a space for the cord between them.
Form a second groove in the same way, at right angles to the first. The orange now has four quarters outlined. Fill these with cloves. Tie the cord around the orange, neatening the ends to prevent fraying.
Hang in a dry place, such as an airing cupboard or linen closet for a week or two to allow the orange to dry out. Make a mixture of equal parts of allspice and cinnamon. Sprinkle over the pomander. Wrap lightly in a cloth and keep in a dry place for another week.

allspice + cinnamon

Above *These delicate and delightfully fragrant tussie mussies can be made with either fresh or dried flowers. Use them to give an original touch to a dinner table or as an unusual present.*

Tussie Mussies

These little nosegays can be made of either fresh or dried flowers and herbs, but should be as sweet smelling as possible. They were carried up until the eighteenth century both for their perfume to ward off the evil smells which abounded—and also because they were thought to be a protection against infection. And in England judges still carry a traditional Tussie Mussie made up of herbs.

There are endless variations of herbs or flowers which can be used to make up a Tussie Mussie. Usually, however, you start with a small flower like a rose-bud, round it you put feathery silvery leaves like Artemisia or Centaurea Maritima and tie the bunch with wool or strong cotton thread. Around this put a circle of Marjoram or Thyme, then a round of Mint, Lavender or Rosemary, then perhaps Lemon Balm and a row of Astrantia flowers. Finish off with a circle of Geranium or Sage leaves and tie the whole tightly. It is worth remembering that if they are made with freshly-picked herbs, Tussie Mussies will dry well and keep their scent, so they make delightful presents. While for an unusual touch to a dinner party you could put a tiny Tussie Mussie by each place setting.

Pressed flowers

Pressing flowers is a charming pastime that can be enjoyed by all age groups. All sorts of unusual and original objects can be made—from greeting cards and calendars to pictures and wall plaques used as a delightful memorial to a special holiday, picnic or a favourite garden.

Selecting material for pressing

When trying to decide what to press, it is best to try everything and learn what works, and what does not, by experience. Some flowers can change colour badly or lose their colour altogether.

Others will fade but still look very attractive in an arrangement of muted and soft tones.

From the garden many flowers can be used and nothing is lost by experimenting with varieties not mentioned. Pansies in particular are effective, retaining their beautiful bright colours during pressing. Other well-tried favourites are hydrangea, larkspur, edelweiss, gentian, primrose, chionodoxia, hypernicum, montbretia, honeysuckle, leucheria and sedum. But others such as marigolds, anchusa, verbascum, nasturtium and delphinium, geranium and clematis,

There are many varieties of flowers which take well to pressing.
Below right The delicate and rare flowers of the edelweiss.
Below The colourful poppy. This will often turn a dark rust when being pressed.
Bottom The bright colours of the pansy makes them ideal subjects for pressing.

hellebore and euphorbia all take well to pressing.

The country also provides a wealth of material. But remember, if gathering wild flowers have a responsible attitude to the plants found there. Only pick what you know you are really going to use and certainly do not pick anything that you know to be rare or in danger of extinction. If in any doubt over a particular flower or plant, leave it alone and check first. Various environmental departments publish charts that will help you in this. If in a field of buttercups, take as many as you like, but if you find a single orchid, leave it to establish itself and restrain your collecting instincts for a few years. Remember that the humble daisy or buttercup will press as well and look as good as do the most exotic of flowers.

Picking flowers for pressing

The best time to pick flowers for pressing is on a dry sunny day. If the blooms are at all damp, pressing will leave dark patches on the petals and leaves.

Flowers picked in the garden cause little difficulty and can be brought directly indoors and prepared for pressing. In the countryside, however, picking is not so easy especially as wild flowers tend to wilt and die very quickly. Therefore, if out looking for specimens, take a book and some absorbent paper and press as you pick.

Alternatively, take a plastic bag with a rubber band to secure the opening to carry your specimens home in. But press them as soon as possible.

Pressing flowers

The actual process of pressing flowers

Below The primrose family, with the pale delicate colour of the wild primrose to the bright red and purple of its cultivars, provides a wealth of colour for the enthusiast.

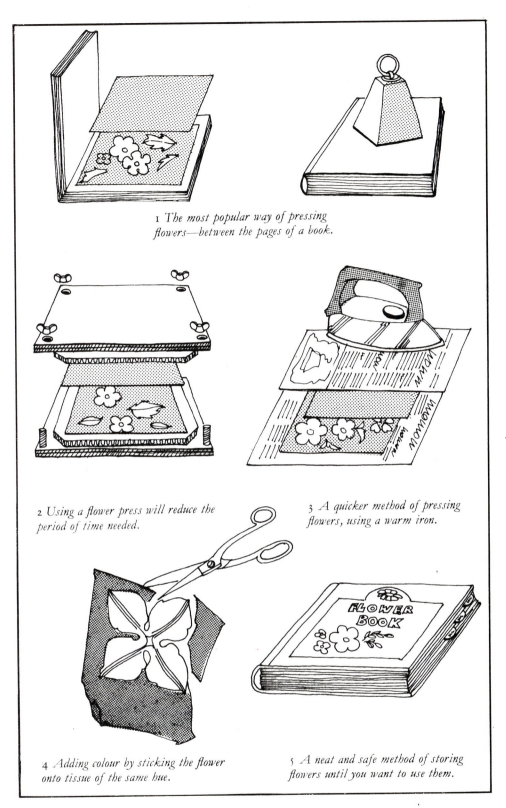

1 *The most popular way of pressing flowers—between the pages of a book.*

2 *Using a flower press will reduce the period of time needed.*

3 *A quicker method of pressing flowers, using a warm iron.*

4 *Adding colour by sticking the flower onto tissue of the same hue.*

5 *A neat and safe method of storing flowers until you want to use them.*

is quite simple, but it is also a hobby which requires some patience otherwise an effective design can be spoilt by the rotting away of a flower which has not been properly dried.

To preserve flowers in any form you must first extract the moisture. With pressed flowers the moisture is removed by placing the plant between absorbent sheets of paper, then sliding this sandwich of flowers very carefully between the pages of a suitable book. Those with absorbent pages such as an old telephone directory make excellent pressed flower retainers. At all costs avoid using books with non-absorbent glossy pages.

White blotting paper is the most absorbent surface to use—it can be dried and used again and again. If, however, you do not want to go to the expense of buying blotting paper until you have decided if you are going to enjoy the craft, then you can use several layers of toilet tissue very successfully. Kitchen towel is not advisable because its textured pattern is transferred to the plant material.

Whatever paper you decide upon, having made your sandwich of flowers, place at intervals throughout your book until it is full (allowing sufficient thickness between the pages to preserve a flat surface).

Finish by placing a heavy weight on the top to assist the flowers in keeping their shape—and to help extract the moisture. An old iron, kitchen scale weight, or even a brick will serve this purpose adequately.

Leave the flowers in this press for at least three weeks without disturbing them, being sure to resist the temptation to observe their progress.

An alternative method of pressing is to buy a flower press. Those on the market tend to be child-sized and therefore quite small, so if serious about the hobby and the number of books lying around the house is limited, you can make one yourself. Instructions for this are given on page 70.

Using a press will reduce the pressing time as the plants may be removed after they have been in the press one week, rehoused in fresh blotting paper and placed in a book, with a weight, for a further week.

If, however, you wish to use your material quicker than this, then place your sandwich of paper between newspaper or material and, using an iron set at heat mark 'wool', press firmly—thereafter, remove to a book with a weight and place in a warm cupboard [closet] overnight.

Hints and tips for pressing

Having chosen the flowers to press and made sure that they are dry, the process is easy, but care must be taken to achieve the best results.

Stalks As the stalks of most flowers become hard and brittle when dry it is necessary to snip the flower heads off the stalks near the top. The stalks of the daisy press extremely well and so a supply of these can often be pressed and used in designs for other plants.

Flower heads Gently press the centre of the flowers (the thickest part) between the fingers and place it face downwards onto the pressing paper, leaving plenty of room between each flower.

Very large flowers or flowers with petals overlapping are often best pressed petal by petal and then reassembled later.

Stems Do not attempt to straighten the stem but allow them to curve naturally. These lines, as in fresh flower arrangements, will be a great help to you when forming a design.

Storing pressed flowers

Whatever method you use, when you are completely satisfied that your material is dry, remove it from the press as further prolonged pressure may impair it.

Using tweezers the material can then be removed and stored in a box with a cellophane lid or, failing this, transferred to an ordinary box with one of the flowers taped to the lid for easy identification.

A good method of storing flowers is to leave the flowers in blotting paper inside an old wall-paper book, keeping each species together. The book can then be indexed with protruding tabs of card for easy and quick selection.

Colour retention

Unfortunately most colours will fade in time, but you can help prevent this or turn it to your advantage. A few hints are listed below.

Avoid placing your picture on a sunny wall as the sun will fade them.

Choose backgrounds carefully so that, when the natural colours do eventually fade, they will still look attractive. Grasses often turn a golden colour and flowers sometimes take a creamy shade of brown. With a good design and the right backcloth, the mellowed picture can be just as attractive as when it had vibrant colour, if not more so.

Another way to help is to stick the flowers onto a tissue paper base of the same hue as the flowers' natural colour. Cut around the outline with a pair of sharp pointed scissors, and then use in the normal way.

The flowers can also be painted with water coloured paints. You may experience some difficulty in getting the paint to adhere since plants sometimes become water repellent when dry. So use a little liquid soap mixed with your paints to overcome this.

It is possible to change the colours of flowers, or enhance their own natural colour, by slitting the stem slightly and placing the stem in a strong ink dye—the flower will draw up the dye as it would water. The success of this method varies according to flowers and conditions.

Pressing flowers is a charming pastime which can be enjoyed by all age groups. The only real requirement is patience although there are some ways of speeding up the pressing process, but this does not always make for successful results.

Making a flower press

Making a simple flower press.

1 Smooth all surfaces and edges of the plywood with sandpaper.

2 Mark the position of the bolts on the diagonals.

3 Drill the holes for the bolts, using waste timber as a base.

4 Pushing the bolts through, tap gently with a hammer until the square shank has engaged fully with the plywood.

5 Assemble your 'sandwich' on the baseboard.

6 The complete press, ready for use.

A small flower press is quite easy to make and is invaluable to the pressed flower enthusiast or those with little room to spare. The simple flower press shown below can be made in the suggested size or the measurements can be altered to take more flowers.

Materials

2 pieces of 9mm ($\frac{3}{8}$in) plywood, 30cm × 30cm (12 in × 12in)

4 6mm ($\frac{1}{4}$in) coach bolts [tap bolts], 7·5cm (3in) long

4 wing nuts and 4 washers to fit

7 pieces of double faced corrugated cardboard 29cm × 29cm (11$\frac{1}{2}$in × 11$\frac{1}{2}$in)

12 pieces of blotting paper 29cm × 29 cm (11$\frac{1}{2}$in × 11$\frac{1}{2}$in)

Tools

Coarse sandpaper and block
Sharp pencil and rule
Waste timber [lumber scraps]
Hand drill and 6·5mm ($\frac{1}{4}$in) or 8mm ($\frac{5}{16}$in) bit
Hammer
Trimming knife or scissors.

To make up

Start by smoothing all the surfaces, edges and corners of the plywood, using the sandpaper wrapped around a block.

Using the pencil and rule, draw

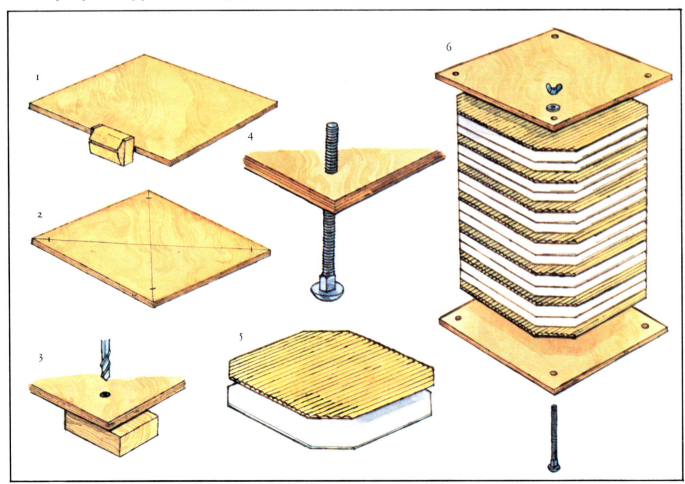

diagonal lines on each board and measure in about 3cm (1¼in) from each corner. This is the centre of the holes.

Drill eight holes, (4 for each board) to take the bolts. Press the plywood hard on to the waste timber when you are drilling so you don't drill through your work surface and to avoid splitting the plywood.

Push the bolts through the holes in one piece of plywood and tap them home with a hammer until the square shank has engaged fully with the wood.

Trim your pieces of corrugated cardboard and blotting paper to the exact size and trim off their corners, to avoid the bolts.

Assemble your 'sandwich' on the baseboard. Put two sheets of blotting paper between each layer of cardboard to press the flowers between and then thread the bolts through the holes in the top board, add washers and screw down the wing nuts.

Simple projects

Although working with pressed flowers is fairly simple, some delightful, original objects can be made which would enhance any home or which could be given as gifts. Below are some suggestions for quick projects which will give the beginner some experience in dealing with pressed flower designs.

To make a calendar

You will need six varieties of pressed flowers to represent the months in which they flower. Obviously this would need planning ahead. Snowdrops and crocus could be chosen for the winter months, daffodils and tulips for spring, roses and pansies for summer and Michaelmas daisies for autumn.

Six sheets of stiff white card (plain index cards would be ideal)
Clear, sticky-backed, [adhesive] plastic sheet
A rubber-based adhesive [rubber cement]
Ribbon
Calendar booklet

Making up

Cut out the stiff white card to size and group the flowers of choice loosely at first. Play around with them on the card until the arrangement is balanced and pleasing to the eye. This should be done carefully so as to prevent any damage to the flowers. Tweezers can be used to make the job

Below Some of the simple yet attractive projects that can be made using pressed flowers in conjunction with clear sticky backed plastic. Book marks, cards and stationery can all be given a personal touch in this way.

easier when dealing with really delicate flowers. When the arrangement is ready, dab some adhesive very lightly onto the backs of the flowers to stick them down. Do not, however, use too much, as this can discolour the flowers.

Cut the clear, sticky-backed plastic [adhesive] sheeting into the shape of the calendar plus 2·5cm (1in) all round. Very carefully stick it over the card. The backing needs to be removed a little at a time as it is placed over the work, as the plastic can make the flowers move about. Ensure that there are no air bubbles trapped underneath and then fold over the edges.

Punch two holes through the top of each card and thread the cards together with ribbon. Attach a calendar to the bottom of the back card with two strips of ribbon.

Obviously there are numerous variations on this simple project. The card can be of any size and of any colour which would enhance the natural beauty of the flowers. If a soft fabric is to be used as a background, it should be cut at least 5cm (2in) larger than the card on each side and then laced across the back. Felt is a good medium as it only needs to be cut to the exact size. If you want a very neat finish, stick a piece of cartridge paper over the joins at the back.

Adapting this sort of project is quite easy. For instance greetings cards can be fun to make and pressed flowers add a touch of individuality to the simplest message. Or writing paper can be given a personal touch by such additions.

Book marks can also be made quite simply by adapting the basic principle used above to make the calendar, using card and clear sticky-backed [adhesive] plastic. However, a much neater finish can be achieved by using strips of film.

To make a book mark
Beg or buy some strips of 35mm film from a processing camera shop. If these are black, exposed and developed films they can be used as a background but the top piece must be transparent. Undeveloped film, which is opaque, can be cleared by dipping it into Hypo.

Cut two strips of film, one clear and one dark, each measuring 15cm (6in).

Mount the flowers on the background with adhesive, cover with the clear film and then lace cord, ribbon or embroidery threads through the holes along the edge of the film.

Finish at either end with a neat tassel and seal the bookmark top and bottom with a little adhesive.

CALENDAR

Pressed flower pictures

Opposite page A simple but effective design based on a central point. Loose petals have been made up into a false flower using a daisy as the flower centre.

One of the most popular ways of using pressed flowers is to make a picture with them—a memory of the beautiful flowers chosen from your garden perhaps, a day in the country or a memorable holiday. Whatever the reason, a picture is the culmination of the happy hours spent in collecting and pressing your specimens.

Choosing a frame

New frames can be bought from most department stores or handicraft centres either complete or in kits ready for you to assemble. You might, however, be lucky enough to pick one up at a jumble sale or junk shop and, for a small outlay restore it to its former beauty. All you need is sandpaper and a pot of paint. If glass has to be bought, you may like to try non-reflecting glass which gives the pressed flowers a more life-like appearance.

Backings and backcloths

The backing of the frame is usually made of hardboard but thick cardboard will do the job equally well. Panel pins [tacks] will be needed to hold the back-ing firmly against the glass to avoid any movement in the frame or to allow air to seep in and spoil the flowers.

The material for the backing can be almost anything from paper to silks. Pressed flowers stand out well on a black or white background. Choose the background carefully so that when the natural colours do eventually fade, they will still look attractive. Grasses often turn a golden colour and flowers to a brown or creamy colour, so if you have a good design on the right backcloth, the mellowed picture can be just as attractive, if not more so in some cases.

Making up

Having assembled all your materials on a clean working surface, remove the glass from the frame, slip it into a pad of newspaper and safely put to one side. Line the backing with white paper and then with your backing material and return to the empty frame. By doing this you will prevent making the common mistake of allowing your design to flow under the inside edge of the frame.

The design for your picture largely depends on the shape of your frame.

Right Pressed flowers lend themselves naturally to designs based on curves. For this reason, designs based upon arcs and ovals are particularly success-ful. To obtain the curved line a plate of the right size can be used as a guide. Far right Designs based on a geometric shape can also be effective. By removing the flowers completely from their stems, a point from which the design will flow can be built up on the base line of a triangle.

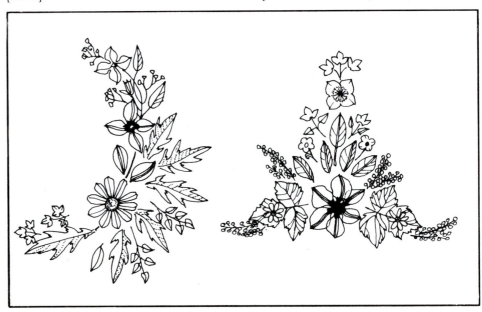

Ideas can be found on postcards, greeting cards or birthday cards. Try not to overcrowd your picture and arrange large flowers and strong colours to the centre of the design, with some of the buds on the outside. Use the natural curves of the stems, and make the flowers and leaves look as if they are growing and not suspended in mid-air, unless of course you are making a symmetrical design.

It is often a good idea not to glue the design down but simply cover it with a piece of glass and leave to the next day, when you may want to alter it.

As with most designs a rubber-based adhesive [rubber cement] is the best to use as it rolls easily off the fingers, the flowers and most materials. But do use it sparingly as too much will impair the life of the flowers and the glass, if fitted tightly against the flowers, will keep the design in place even without glue.

When you are satisfied with your design, remove it from the frame and put it to one side, protecting it with a clean piece of blotting paper and a light weight. Turn the frame over and using a measure and pencil, mark down each side equally where you want the picture hooks to go. Bore a small hole with a gimlet and then it will be a simple matter to screw the hooks in place when the picture is assembled.

Clean the glass carefully, holding it by the outside edge to prevent smearing with finger marks, then place it over the design. Holding the two pieces together firmly, insert them into the frame. Before securing with panel pins, make one last check that no loose bits have escaped and need removing—a baby's hair brush is an excellent tool for doing this.

Complete the picture with panel pins, hooks and wire and neaten off the back with paper. Place on a sunless wall to avoid premature fading.

Above A design based on a central point and given a curved shape by the use of an oval border. Whole cultivated flowers are used as the pivot and leaves and wild flowers used to trail off from the centre.

Right 'Iceberg' by Pamela McDowell uses stems to give a wonderfully flowing line to the design. White rose petals, pressed separately, were used for the two central flowers and the undersides of raspberry leaves for the arc.

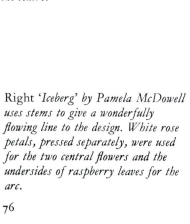

Left *Wild flowers can be just as effective as those grown in the garden. Rosebay willow herb, poppies and yarrow have all been pressed and made up into this splendid collage. The whole design is based on a board with leaded glass mounted in the frame.*

Flowers under glass

Opposite page A small wine table can be made in a stand with a recess deep enough to take a thin backing material and glass, cut out of the centre. It is important that the glass fits tightly otherwise air will seep in and ruin the flowers.

The flowers in the place mats have taken on a delicate hue, blending perfectly with the backing material. Below An attractive after-dinner tray with a bright arc design of montbretia and sedum.

The basic principles of using pressed flowers under glass are all fundamentally the same whether used for a picture, tray or place mat. Glass not only makes the flowers look more attractive but also, by protecting them from wear and tear, enables them to be used to decorate practical items.

To make the tray

The size you make the tray is really a matter of personal choice, but as a guide, a large tray of 42cm (17in) diameter is suitable for after-dinner use

with fruit, nuts and cheese; a 35cm (14in) diameter for cheese and biscuits and a 30cm (12in) diameter for bottles and glasses. Hardboard makes an ideal material to use for the base.

You will also need a flexible strip of thin wood to bend around the outside of the tray to form a rim. This is then glued and pinned to form a neat join. The strip must be just deep enough to cover the depth of the hardboard base and the glass together.

The whole tray is then completed with a wide furnishing braid. Choose one with a fluted edge so that this can be glued over the rim and on to the glass making an attractive finish and covering up any joins.

Complete the tray by attaching felt to the underside of the base to avoid scratching a polished table.

The design

To make a symmetrical design, measure your pattern out accurately, and use an uneven number of flowers to start with. Work out the idea on paper first and then measure and dot the material with a pencil where you want the flowers to go.

The design on the tray illustrated is based on dark green velvet backing. A guideline for the crescent is made by pressing a plate on to the velvet and then following the impression with an outline of bleached, glycerined and pressed choisya leaves. Only half the circle is necessary for the crescent; the remaining half can then be easily smoothed away with the fingers.

Once you have got the basic shape, it is then fairly simple to arrange stalks and flowers to look as if they are flowing from it.

To make the place mats

Making a place mat is similar to making a tray, but you will not need a rim. Although they can be made very successfully out of wood, cork is more

Right A decorative border around a mirror gives a delightfully feminine touch to any room.
Below Door finger plates using summer flowers mounted under glass. To make the finger plates, cut white cardboard to the size of a perspex finger plate and position the flowers and stalks. Stick the flowers down gently with a rubber-based adhesive [rubber cement] and cover with the perspex plate.

satisfactory medium as it will absorb the heat better.

It is wise to choose a circular shape for the mat if you intend to protect it with glass. A glazier can cut this shape out with a special tool, but has to cut an oval out by hand, making it much more expensive.

Using the glass or mat as a template, cut out circles of thin white card and glue on to the cork base, then add a backing material of your choice. Cream or white embroidery linen makes a good background for the flowers and will match any colour scheme. A pretty braid can be bought in a haberdashery [notions] department, to hold the layers together and give an attractive finish.

Always ensure that the glass is spotless before placing it over the pressed flowers, and check before sealing the layers together that no loose fragments have escaped.

To seal the layers of mat and glass together before glueing on the braid, use narrow adhesive tape. This will help prevent any liquid seeping under the braid and spoiling the flowers.

Mirror

Add a pretty border to a mirror—it's quite simple to make and gives a delightfully feminine air to any room. The method is similar to making a pressed flower picture only instead of working on a matt background, you are using a mirror as your base.

Materials

You will need a frame with a deep recess as it will have to take a sheet of mirror as well as the picture glass and the card or wood backing. If you have bought a frame with glass already cut, it is quite easy to buy some mirror cut to the same size. If not, measure the width and length of the backing and purchase both glass and mirror to the required size.

The design

Make your design on paper first to prevent making mistakes later. The glue used on a shiny surface should be a contact adhesive which dries quickly and does not allow for last minute changes.

Ensure that as you make your design, none of the flowers will later be concealed by the frame.

Use the glue sparingly and quickly clean away the excess with turpentine.

When dry, carefully fit the glass over the mirror and, holding firmly, place inside the frame. Place the backing firmly on top and secure using a strong masking tape.

Flowers under varnish

One of the problems in dealing with pressed flowers is their tendency to fade if kept in strong light. However, there are ways of counteracting this process and, with care, the most spectacular effects can be achieved, using light to emphasize the shape, structure and colour of your dried materials.

To make a lampshade
A lampshade is one of the more successful ways of combining flowers and light and the risks of fading can be minimized by using a low-wattage smoked bulb in the lamp.

Choose the shape of your shade first and measure around the circumference to find out exactly how much paper you will need. For an average size shade approximately one sheet of opaque paper is usually sufficient. Hand-made Japanese or Chinese paper is ideal, although as it is rather delicate, it should be treated with great care. It is made in a variety of patterned designs, including one with leaves and butterflies already embedded, plain or patterned.

You will also need some white emulsion paint, contact adhesive, alcohol-based wallpaper sealant, scissors and a large paint brush.

The method
First paint the wire frame with one coat of emulsion paint. It is possible to buy a frame already painted but it is a simple task to paint your own. When dry, lay the frame down on to the paper and cut a rough shape a little larger than required. If your shade is made up of sections it is best to work each section separately.

The design
Try to visualize how your materials will look when held up to the light. Often it is best to use single flowers and leaves as overlapping materials cause a much darker effect. One flower or leaf, although simple, will give a much more delightful and attractive effect.

Having worked out your design, transfer it to the lampshade paper.

Using the sealant
The advantage of using a wallpaper sealant is that this will adhere the flowers to the paper without using a glue which could mar the design. Apply the sealant thinly but evenly over the side of the paper which will form the outside of the shade. Try to avoid overlapping marks as these will show up when the light is on. For this reason use a large paint brush and try to cover as large an area as possible with one brush stroke.

Apply a thin layer to the back of your pressed materials, and lay them gently on to the paper. Carefully, seal the lampshade all over covering the dried materials. Ensure that there are no air pockets either under or around the edges of your materials. Allow to dry and then add another coat.

Making up
Section by section, depending upon the shape of your frame, fix the paper to the shade. To do this use a contact adhesive. As the glue will dry quickly, the paper must be placed accurately. Fix the top first and then the sides. Pull the whole section taut from the bottom and trim the surplus paper. Repeat the process for all sections.

When all the sides have been positioned on the frame, give the whole shade one more covering with sealant. This not only strengthens the paper but also gives the shade a more translucent look and secures the flowers more firmly. Later if the flowers begin to fade, it is possible to tint them again by painting them with water colours and a brush dipped in liquid detergent and then resealing.

Finally, as a finishing touch, make a line of glue around the top and bottom of the shade and affix some velvet ribbon.

Above *The method used for decorating a lampshade can also be used for all manner of articles. Boxes and lids can be given a decorative touch or a plaque can be made although a more attractive finish can be made by the method shown overleaf.*

Opposite *The finished lampshade, made up using paper with butterflies and leaves already embedded. A similar effect can be achieved with your own design by using plain or patterned paper with a wallpaper sealant.*

Decoupage with flowers

Very simply, the word 'decoupage' means working with paper cut-outs, sticking them on to a prepared surface and then covering them with layers of varnish. The designer of this original wall plaque has taken this basic idea and replaced the paper cut-outs with pressed flowers. These have a similar but more delicate texture to paper when dried.

To make the wall plaque

To make a wall plaque, first select a suitable piece of wood about 1·3cm (½in) thick, and cut into the desired shape. A good 'do-it-yourself' hardware shop will often have off-cuts of wood which they will select and cut into shape for you. The wood must be smooth and sealed with varnish before starting the design. If the natural grain of the wood does not suit your design, the plaque could also be stained before sealing.

As with all pressed flower designs, the position of the flowers should be worked out on paper first and then stuck down on the plaque using a rubber-based adhesive [rubber cement].

Every part of the plant material must be glued down securely to avoid movement when the first coat of varnish is applied. Press the flowers down firmly with a small damp pad of cotton wool, being careful to remove any excess glue, and then leave overnight to dry.

Colouring the design

Flowers under varnish will need to be coloured. There are exceptions, of course, such as the glycerined and bleached choisya leaves which retain their beautiful golden colour. Water paints are ideal for this. However, when the moisture has been extracted from plant material, it becomes water repellent and will reject the paint. To overcome this, make a strong solution of liquid detergent and water. Dip your paint brush into this solution as you would in the normal way with plain water, before coating your brush with paint.

Varnishing the plaque

Many layers of clear varnish are now applied, either gloss, semi-gloss or matt depending on choice.

At least five coats of varnish need to be applied and allowed to dry before sanding the surface, then the smoothing process can begin. To do this you will require fine sandpaper (400 or 600), and steel wool (ooo) gauge. Both the steel wool and sandpaper are used wet and dry.

With a circular movement first use the sandpaper and then the steel wool, dry, removing particles of dust between each process with a damp cloth. Then repeat the smoothing method with the sandpaper after first dipping it into a little warm soapy water, clean with a damp cloth, and use the same method with the steel wool.

When drying, polish with an old nylon stocking rolled into a ball. The nylon in the stocking will pick up any bits and find the snags in the wood which will need further sanding.

Repeat the sanding method between applying coats of varnish until the flowers are embedded well enough into the varnish to leave the surface smooth and even to the touch.

If you use a matt varnish, the appearance will be dull. If the effect is not pleasing, it is a simple matter to add another coat of varnish with a different finish.

To complete the plaque, attach a piece of felt or material to the back to avoid scratching the wall, and screw a ring into the top of the wood to hang the plaque by.

This idea can be extended to cover all manner of articles—from adding a delicate touch to wooden furniture (similar to inlaid flowers in many Victorian designs) to decorating boxes and door finger plates.

Opposite The designer of this original wall plaque has taken the basic idea of decoupage and replaced the usual paper cutouts with pressed flowers. These are then covered with layers of varnish until the whole plaque is smooth to the touch.

Paperweights

One of the most attractive ways to preserve a dried or pressed flower is to set it in or behind sparkling glass or plastic. There are two main methods of doing this, one simple for pressed flowers, and one demanding more expert skills, for both dried and pressed flowers.

Pressed flowers paperweights
Buy a plain glass paperweight and place it on a sheet of thin card. Trace around the base and then cut out the shape 0.5cm (¼in) inside the drawn line. Cover the card with a suitable fabric and arrange and mount the flowers in an attractive design.

Cut a circle of felt the same size as the base of the paperweight. Apply adhesive around the edge of the circle of felt and stick on the bottom of the covered card. The sticky edge of the felt can then be pressed against the glass base of the paperweight and the edges trimmed neatly.

Embedding flowers in plastic
This method is slightly more technical than most projects but the result is an eye-catching and unusual three D effect and the idea can be extended to make many other decorative items such as door finger plates, pendants and candle holders. The only real skills required are that you must follow instructions carefully and be prepared to experiment a little to create unusual and beautiful effects. The basic method is that some polyester resin is mixed with hardener and poured into a suitable mould to form a thin layer of liquid. The resin takes between thirty minutes and three hours to become gelatinous and sticky to the touch. Another layer is poured and the procedure repeated until the mould is full. The object to be encased is placed on top of a layer when the resin has become gelatinous and just before the next layer is poured. Some distortion may be noticeable when the cast is viewed from the side and along the layers of resin. Therefore, always design the casting so that you will usually look at it at right angles to the layers of resin.

Materials
Polyester resin and hardener are obtainable from most art shops and a number of toy shops. The resin, a clear liquid, is available in tins ranging in size from 340g to 5 kilos (12oz-11lb). The liquid hardener is bought in polythene bottles with a measure marked on the outside.

Moulds can be bought from many art shops. They range from cube and cylindrical shapes to intricately-shaped ones for making jewellery. But it is not always necessary to purchase moulds, as you can often improvise with cups, bowls, dishes or small trays. A mould should ideally be made of soft, pliable plastic such as that used for refrigerator containers. It is easier to remove the hardened resin from soft plastic moulds because the plastic 'gives', allowing the block to be squeezed out. On no account use any containers made of rigid, brittle plastic or polystyrene foam, for there is a strong likelihood of the resin reacting with the plastic. Most other materials, such as wood, glass or metal are suitable, provided you can get the block out of them afterwards.

Wax polish (not a silicone type) is used as a 'release agent' to coat the inside of the mould and prevent the resin from sticking to it. Paper cups or yoghourt cartons are ideal for mixing the resin and hardener in, as they can be thrown away afterwards. Cheap, disposable spatulas or ice-cream spoons are ideal for stirring the mixture. A bottle of dry-cleaning fluid or acetone is needed to remove spots of resin from tabletops or clothes.

Other tools needed are a soft plastic jug with a scale marked on it, a pair of tweezers if you are encasing delicate objects, wet and dry sandpapers ranging from coarse to very fine, some metal

Embedding a flower in plastic
1 *First pour.*
2 *Object embedded in second pour.*
3 *Resin or felt base.*

polish or special polishing paste, and a small sheet of glass.

Embedding flowers

Before embedding, the flowers must first be dried by the air drying method (page 24). Flowers or grasses in resin may produce small air bubbles so when pouring layers of resin round the flowers, pour the layer so that it comes only two thirds of the way up the flower. Any bubbles can then escape upwards before the next pouring.

Safety first

Once set, polyester resin is non-toxic and non-inflammable. But when it is in a liquid form it is inflammable and gives off a vapour which is harmful if breathed in large quantities. Therefore, always take the following precautions, and in all cases follow the manufacturer's instructions.

Keep the room well ventilated and do not inhale the fumes given off by the liquid resin. Be especially careful when pouring it into the moulds. Keep the liquid resin away from any naked flames. And finally, keep the hardener away from the eyes and skin as it is corrosive and poisonous. You should use rubber gloves when handling the har-

Below *Flower paperweights made by embedding dried flower heads in plastic. All sorts of items can be made by this method including pendants, door finger plates and candle holders.*

87

dener. If you do spill any, wash it off with luke warm water.

Making a transparent cast

First choose your working area. The reaction between the resin and hardener will take place at any temperature above 15°C (59°F) but 20°C (68°F) is more satisfactory.

Prepare the working area, making sure that there is adequate ventilation in the room. Check with a spirit level [just level] that the working surface is level, otherwise the liquid will not fill the moulds to an even depth all the way across. Cover the working surface with newspaper or cellophane.

Wash and dry the mould and then rub some wax (non-silicone) polish over the inside and polish it. Enough of the wax film will be left on the inside of the mould to prevent the resin from sticking to it.

Place the mould on your level working surface. Then fill the mould with water up to the level the cast is to reach. Pour the water from the mould into the measuring jug and note the volume of water. Empty, then dry, the jug and mould. Fill the jug with resin to just above the level of water reached, so that there is approximately 5% to 10% more resin by volume in the jug than there was water. You need the extra volume of resin as some is certain to remain in the jug when you pour some extra resin into the mould. Then refer to the manufacturer's instructions and add the required amount of hardener to the liquid. This is normally 2%, but the right proportion is marked on the sides of the bottle containing the hardener. Mix thoroughly using the wooden spoon or spatula and stir for at least a minute.

Pouring the resin

Now pour the first layer of resin into the mould and cover the top of the jug and place it in a bowl of cold water. This will prevent it from hardening before you use it again. The depth of this and following layers can vary within a considerable margin. The depth is regulated by the fact that the setting resin heats up. If the layer is too thick, too little heat will escape from the mould and there will be a build-up of heat that will crack the resin. This is particularly disastrous if you want a perfectly transparent cast. Alternatively, when the layers, and therefore, the finished product, are too thin, it may crack. Keep the layers between 3-13mm ($\frac{1}{8}$-$\frac{1}{2}$in) thick. Allow the resin to begin to set. The

time needed depends on a number of variables. The thinner the layer of resin, the more hardener there is mixed with the resin, and the higher the room temperature, the quicker the resin will begin to gel and become thick and sticky to touch. The resin may remain tacky for about 20 minutes, so it is important to check at regular intervals how far the setting has progressed. Use a clean wooden spoon to check. Do not be afraid of leaving a mark if the resin has partially set; it has the convenient property of 'closing up' after the surface has been disturbed.

When embedding flowers or adding another layer of resin they should be added when the resin has become tacky, but not hard. Embedding objects in the cast is done simply by placing the object on top of one layer of resin. It will not sink in. As many layers as necessary are then poured until the object is completely covered.

Removing the mould

When the last layer of resin has been poured leave it to set for as long as possible; preferably overnight but for at least eight hours in any case. Flexible plastic moulds are easy to remove as the 'give' allows the casting to be eased out. If the casting does stick, carefully run a thin-bladed knife round the edges.

China, glass or metal moulds must first be put in very hot water for at least 10 minutes and then plunged directly into cold water and left there for 10 minutes. If available, ice cubes should be added to the water to keep it cool. Then remove the mould, hold it upside down and tap it gently against a table top. The cast should slip out easily. If it does not and the mould is still slightly warm, put it back in the cold water for a little longer.

If the last, or bottom layer, of resin has set rough, it should be smoothed. Wrap a fairly coarse piece of wet and dry paper around a flat sided block of wood. Wet the paper and smooth the base of the casting, moving the block in small circles. Use successively finer grades of paper until the base is smooth all over. This will produce a flat eggshell finish which can be an attractive base of a number of castings. If a clear sparkling finish is needed, metal polish or special polishing paste for resin should be applied, and then rubbed with a soft duster.

The surface of the cast is fairly robust, but as the resin continuous to harden for a few weeks it is best to treat it carefully to begin with.

Above *Be careful not to trap air bubbles when embedding intricate pieces.*

Pictures supplied by
H. Allen: 23(r)
Amateur Gardening: 19(t)
D. Arminson: 21(bl), 66
J. Banks: 21(br)
Steve Bicknell: 43, 50, 88
M. Boys: 24/5, 36/100   Idees: 68
R. J. Corbin: 11(t), 16(tr)
C. J. Dawkins: 21(t)
Pamela McDowell: 76(r), 80
J. E. Downward: 11(b)
Alan Duns: 40, 58, 71, 72, 73, 77, 78, 79,
   80/1, 85, 87 /The Flower House: 45, 46
Family Circle: 56(r)
V. Finnis: 14(cl)
Melvin Grey: 47
Steve Herr: 56(l)
M. Holford: 7
Chris Holland: 29
P. Hunt: 16(b), 19(bl)
A. J. Huxley: 20
L. Johns: 31, 42(t), 55, 57
Chris Lewis: 8, 17, 18, 41, 44, 49
Bill McLaughlin: 42(b), 48, 61, 62
J. Markham: 16(tl)
Dick Miller: 27, 35(t)
Keith Morris: 38/9

Tony Page: 34/5, 51, 83
Reproduced by Gracious Permission of
Her Majesty Queen Elizabeth II: 6
Sale Stone Senior: 9
Kim Sayer: 52, 53, 75
H. Smith: 12, 13, 14(t,cr,bl), 15, 16(cl), 22,
   23 65(l,br)
V. Stevenson: 19(br), 50
Sungravure: 59
L. Whicher: 65(tr)
Elizabeth Whiting: 76(l)
M. Wickham: 26, 39(b), 64
ZEFA: 82

We would like to thank the following:
p. 75: Flower picture from Fortnum &
Mason
p. 78: Flower tray designed by
Moyna McWilliam
p. 79: Wine table designed by
Moyna McWilliam
p. 85: Wall plaques designed by
Moyna McWilliam
p. 87: Flower paper weights from
Liberty & Co. Ltd.